*Eog,
i wish ... very best
luck + love
Nee 7/1/2012.*

LITTLE JOHN NEE

A Donegal Trilogy

LITTLE JOHN NEE

A Donegal Trilogy

Published
An Grianán Theatre, Letterkenny, Ireland
www.angrianan.com

Editor
Daithí Ramsay

Assistant Editor
Nicola Burns

Irish Language Editing
Dónall McGinley and Traolach O' Fionnain

Written by
Little John Nee © 2011
The Derry Boat, Rural Electric and The Mental

Photography
Paul McGuckin, except workshop photos
(pages 44–46) by Kate Brown

Design
Carton LeVert, Rathmullan, County Donegal, Ireland

Printed
Browne Printers, Letterkenny, County Donegal, Ireland

** Jericho by Cathal Ó Searcaigh is reproduced here by kind permission
of the author and his publisher. It appears in 'Out in the Open' first
published in 1997 by Cló Iar-Chonnachta, Conamara, Ireland.*

Contents

This publication is supported by the PEACE III Programme
managed for the Special EU Programmes Body by Donegal
County Council, and Donegal County Council Cultural Services.

The Little John Nee Residency is supported by the PEACE III
Programme managed for the Special EU Programmes
Body by Donegal County Council.

An Grianán Theatre is funded by

Little John Nee would like to thank...

Ironically as an independent artist I am totally dependant on the goodwill, support and dare I say love that I receive from so many people.

I dedicate these three plays to the memory of my parents Mary and Dick Nee. Thank you Patricia McBride, Niall Cranney, Daithí Ramsay, Kate Brown, Guy Barriscale, Laura Sheeran, Nuala Ní Chanainn, Kevin Duffy, Jim Faulkner, Anne Marie Langan, Alex Ferni, Pauric Breathnach, Derval Byrne, Jane Talbot, Fergal Gallagher, Karen Gordon, Mike Regan, Traolach O' Fionnain, Donal O' Kelly, Brendan Hone, Murt Collins and everyone at Solas. Aidan Maguire, Libby Carton. All those who participated in the workshops. The Earagail Arts Festival, Terre Duffy, JoAnne Kilmartin and Fergal O' Boyle, Angela McLaughlin, Denise and Laurence Blake, PJ. Clerkin, Mike Diskin, Anne Mannion, Sean Hannigan at the RCC, Jeremy Howard, Tommy McLaughlin, Margaret Hogan, Paul McGuckin, Cathal O' Searcaigh, Beth Phillips, Connie and Sean Tyrell, James C. Harrold, Marilyn Gaughan, Ayoma Bowe, Peter Pringle and Sunny Jacobs, Ray Yeates and everyone at Axis Ballymun, Roisin McGarr, Tomas Hardiman, Midie Corcorran, the Corbally posse and a host of other shams, Raymond Keane, Maria Fleming, Aidan Wallace, Pat O'Reilly, Helen Lane, Sinead Wallace, Amber Schaeffer, Rob Usher. Hemlock, The Sheils Sisters. The Rynne Family, Bridie Grieves, Susan and Eddie Mc Fadden, Bobby Bradshaw, Amy Bradshaw and Harry Bradshaw, Laura Sheeran, Keeva Holland and Saraswati, and last but not least the audiences, thank yoos.

Forgive me if I forgot to include your name, your kindness has its own reward.

Foreword

Donal O'Kelly, February 2011

Grafton Street, Dublin, the mid-1980s. The first thing you would hear was the laughter. Then you would see the massed crowd. If you stood on tippytoes, you might see the Charlie Chaplin figure, singing his heart out and handing a rose to some unsuspecting girl at the front. This was Little John, one of the greatest manipulators of street crowds in the history of street theatre. A man who knew how audiences worked, and who knew how to work them.

Later, he settled in Galway, and I remember bringing my daughter on the crossbar of the bike to Ballygroovy Avenue, the children's theatre venue in a school that Little John ran as part of the Galway Arts Festival.

Later again, I brought both daughters to see The Derry Boat in Sligo, and I can still hear the roars of laughter at the antics of poor oul Little John trying to get a mobile signal in Donegal by standing on top of a barrel.

A couple of years ago, Little John did his first performance of Dead Rooster Blues in my tiny local parish hall in Killargue, Co. Leitrim, as far as I know the only professional theatre show to ever play there.

He performed extracts from The Derry Boat in Glenamoy Hall in Erris, Co Mayo, in support of the people of Rossport opposing the proposed Shell gas pipeline there. He is a regular feature at Pat McCabe's Flatlake Festival, the Electric Picnic, anywhere people are gathered looking for "a bit of craic". Take advice from someone who knows:- don't ever go on after him!

He has for many years been a colossal figure of popular theatre, especially in rural Ireland. He has ploughed his own furrow, created his own artistic path, like Woody Guthrie, through bogs instead of a dustbowl, scattering earthy poetry of the people around him like an Irish Dylan Thomas, and he has opened up fissures in the crust of Irish society in the most subversive way possible – by stealth through entertainment. You could call it the politics of laughter. He holds the mirror up in the funniest way possible. But he still holds the mirror up.

The Derry Boat, dealing as it does with a world of enforced emigration, has special potency now. I'm glad to see that it's touring again. The Mental shines a flickering light, as only Little John can, into a dark and neglected area of recent Irish life, care of the mentally ill. And Rural Electric illuminates and fires up far more than just the houses of the recipients of electricity in 1950s Donegal.

It is a great thing that these plays are published. Performed by Little John, they have engrossed and enthralled audiences all over Ireland for many years in many venues. Sometimes it feels as if, because Little John performs them, and they include songs, the plays themselves are seen, by the "keepers of the canon", as somehow lacking in status. Anyone who reads them, with their poetic flourishes, and their down-to-earth streetwise sense, will know otherwise. They are gems of challenging artistic entertainment, masquerading as just a great night out!

The last time I saw Little John perform, it was in St Nicholas Church in Galway, and he was giving an oration at the funeral service of Pat Bracken, the amazing puppeteer, stonemason, designer and actor who graced the streets and byways of Galway for much of the last twenty years. Little John stressed that Pat was first and foremost an artist, an artist to the core of his being. He said it with conviction born of the knowledge that real artists are sometimes not given due credit by "the powers that be" for their body of work, as in Pat's case. The publication of these plays by An Grianán asserts what many of us have known for a long time, that Little John Nee is an artist to the core of his being, an artist of the highest calibre, and the kind of artist Ireland sorely needs in these seriously trying times. May he march on across the bogs with his theatre torchsongs, and his crowds will, as they have always done, follow him.

Preface

The trump card in Donegal County Council's submission to The Arts Council's Playwrights Commission Scheme in 1998, seeking its support for what was soon to be Little John Nee's most successful work to that point, The Derry Boat, was a curriculum vitae already burgeoning with a host of productions of various sizes and ambition. Most of these were written by John and performed by John, while in others, like the high profile Macnas shows of the late 1980s and early 1990s, John was a central and essential presence.

From the outset though, Donegal and Scotland were always to the fore. Those early productions were populated by a cast of characters who could not possibly have come from anywhere else. The Zen McGonagle, Ghandi of the Gorbals and Jah Kettle were soon joined by Shughie O'Donnell, Joe Boyle, George 'Moody' McLaughlin and Bridie Diver, who in turn may now be ranked alongside Gar O'Donnell, Dolly West, Manus O'Donnell and the Mundy Sisters, as literary creations from the heart of Donegal speaking on a world stage.

Donegal County Council has been delighted, privileged even, to be so closely associated over the past ten years with the rising star that is Little John Nee. John's own career path has mirrored the expansion and coming of age of the cultural sector in Donegal to such an extent that the timing of his Residency at An Grianán Theatre could not have been better. The county is fortunate now to have such a facility, and a team of creative people working therein, who can devise and deliver these initiatives which both serve the needs of creative artist and stimulate, entertain and enthrall the wider community.

It is wonderful to see these three plays – The Derry Boat, The Mental and Rural Electric - in print and published for the first time. It is equally intriguing to imagine how and to where these new stories from Donegal will now travel. Go mba fada is lúcháireach a naistir.

Traolach Ó Fionnáin
Arts Officer, Donegal County Council

Residency

Little John Nee is a creative artist with a singular combination of skills. He is an accomplished writer, actor, storyteller and musician. He has a unique voice, which speaks very clearly about the experience of this corner of our island. He has an excellent ear for the dialects and idioms of speech which are resonant here. However his stories and plays are not parochial, they are filled with humanity, humour and pathos and have a universal appeal.

It has been a real pleasure to work closely with John on this residency and I am extremely proud of the work that he has achieved on the theatre's behalf. A central plank of the programming strategy at An Grianán Theatre since it opened has been to offer a platform to the artists of Donegal and to also to showcase those talents throughout the country. We have successfully achieved this through numerous projects including our own touring productions.

This opportunity arose through Peace III, which was looking for arts projects which would address issues of sectarianism, racism, plus social and geographical isolation in the border communities. I could not think of an artist whose work could more suitably fill that brief. The three plays we selected, which are published here, are particularly relevant to the themes of Peace III.

The residency also created the opportunity for John to share his skills as a creative artist with community groups and other arts practitioners. The workshop programme focused on issues relating to Peace III and did so in a warm and interactive manner making the workshops easily accessible for seniors groups, young people and members of the new communities.

Audiences at performances have been very appreciative and the feedback from the community groups who participated in workshops has been warm and enthusiastic. I am confident that the residency has captured the hearts and minds of the community both here in Donegal and in Derry and Tyrone and has left a lasting legacy of enjoyment and understanding for all those involved.

Patricia McBride
Director, An Grianán Theatre

Workshops

From young immigrant men to Traveller women, secondary school teenagers to university students, HSE clients, older peoples groups and theatre creatives: stories shared are colourful, some are melancholy and others are humorous. In Little John's hands all are precious.

Accompanying Little John as he travelled the potholed highroads and byroads of the Northwest with a ukulele and a well pressed suit jacket on his back has been a real privilege. Renowned in this corner of the island for our hospitality and true to form, we were always greeted with welcoming smiles and a steaming pot of well brewed tea.

The theme, delivery style and format of the workshops undertaken by Little John as part of his residency have varied greatly. This is a measure of the versatile artist he is, adaptable in his approach working with diverse community groups. Though the profile of the group changes from session to session, the constant is Little John's talent of seeing each for who they are, settling down with them and creating a space where an openness and gentleness of story sharing prevails. "It does your heart good," whispered one lady to me as she drained her cup and wiped the tears of laughter from her face.

Workshops linked with the three performances, The Derry Boat, The Mental and Rural Electric, have an emphasis on our shared past and how this influences our cultural identity and sense of belonging. Memories of what times were like for those who travelled on the Derry Boat, who lived and raised families in Scotland, who left families behind in Ireland are recounted from first and second hand experiences by workshop participants.

And of those for whom the Derry Boat itself was not a part of their past, inside the yellow brick walls of St Conals a factor in their present or of those for whom the flame went out when electricity came in; the universal theme of needing to belong is central to all. After seeing The Mental, an elderly gentleman came to me and said: "Thank John for me. It is important that we all see this show." Audiences and workshop participants nod in agreement, laugh in recognition and sigh in the knowledge of a shared understanding. "I have three words," one woman commented: "Light, informative and beauty."

Everyone has a story. I'll share mine and then maybe you might like to share yours. LJN

Kate Brown
February 2011

Credits

DONEGAL RESIDENCY

Producer
Patricia McBride

Publication Editor
Daithí Ramsay

Publication Assistant Editor
Nicola Burns

**"A World Apart"
Exhibition Curators**
Judith McCarthy,
Niamh Brennan and
Caroline Carr

**Education and
Outreach Programme**
Kate Brown

Photography
Paul McGuckin

Production Manager
Niall Cranney

Musicians
Laura Sheeran,
Nuala Ni Chanainn
and Guy Barriscale

Stage Manager
Annemarie Langan

Lighting Designs
Niall Cranney

Technical Assistants
Phil Ruddock and
Paul Kavanagh

**Marketing, P.R. and
Poster Designs**
Daithí Ramsay and
Nicola Burns

Publication Design
Carton LeVert

Administration
Martina Murphy,
Helene McMenamin
and Laura Ferry

THE DERRY BOAT

First Performed
3rd July 1998 in Ramelton Town Hall
as part of the Earagail Arts Festival

Commissioned by
Earagail Arts Festival through the
Arts Council Scriptwriters Award

Written and Performed by
Little John Nee

Directed by
Pauric Breathnach

**Musical score created
and played by**
Fergal Gallagher

Songs by
Little John Nee

Lights by
Pauric Breathnach

Set Design
Pauric Breathnach

Set Built by
Pauric Breathnach and
Fergal Gallagher

Photography
Aengus Mc Mahon

Poster
Larry Hynes A+D

RURAL ELECTRIC

First Performed
9th July 2004 in the Parochial
Hall, Dungloe as part of the
Earagail Arts Festival

Commissioned by
Earagail Arts Festival and the
Donegal County Council Public
Art Programme

Written and Performed by
Little John Nee

Directed by
Little John Nee

**Musical Score Created
and Played by**
Laura Sheeran

Songs
Little John Nee

Lighting Design
Aidan Wallace

Set Design
Mike Regan

Set built by
Mike Regan

Photography
Jane Talbot

THE MENTAL

**Originally Commissioned
and Produced**
May 2006 by Axis, Ballymun
with support from the HSE
North West, Foras Na Gaeilge and
The Arts Council

Written and Directed by
Little John Nee

**Original Score Written
and Performed by**
Laura Sheeran and
Nuala Ni Chanainn

Songs
The Belle of Tir Conaill,
Queen Bee and The Happy
Hour Band written by Little
John Nee, Jericho poem by
Cathal O Searcaigh put to
music by Nuala Ni Chanainn,
The New York songs by The
Mary Duffys.

Musicians
Laura Sheeran and
Nuala Ni Chanainn

Lighting Design
Sinead Wallace

Set Designer
Mike Regan

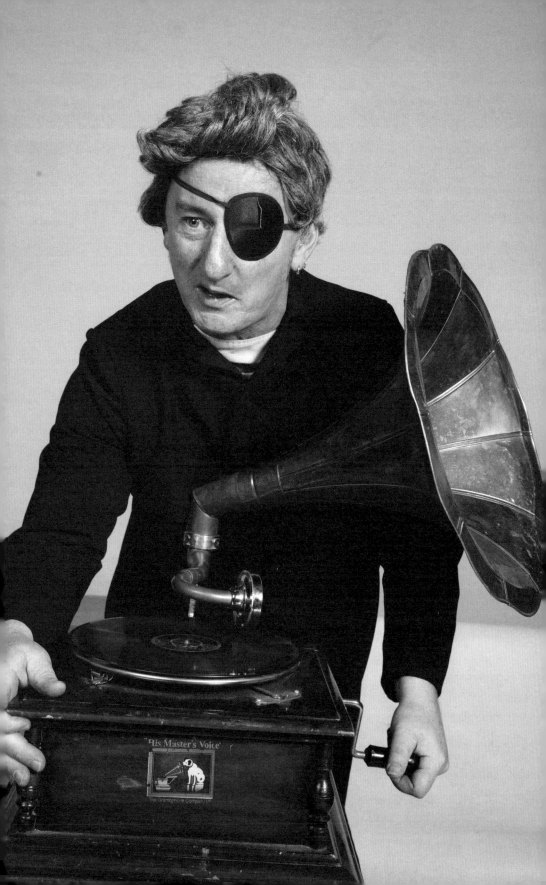

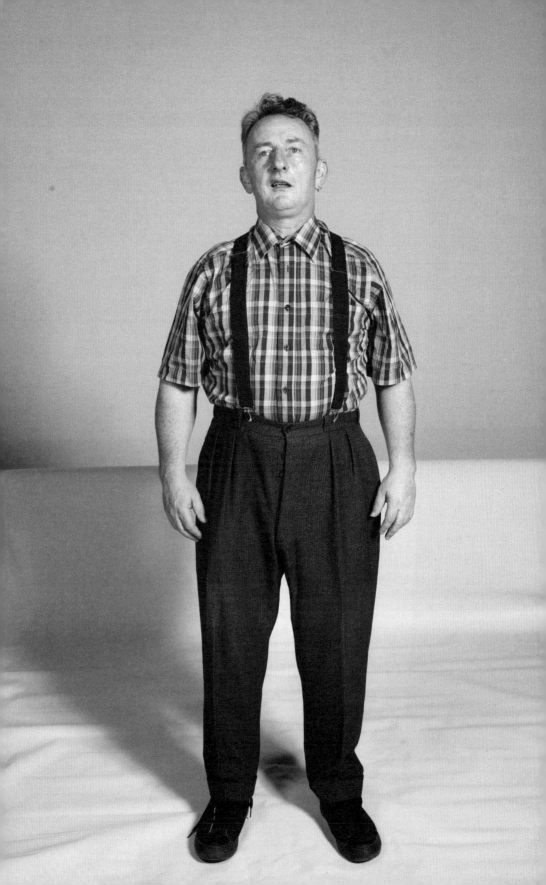

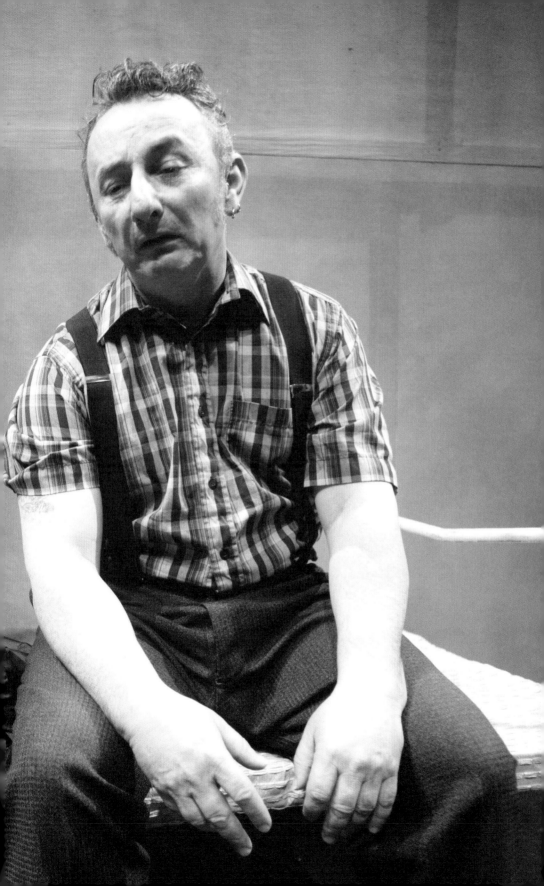

THE PLAYS

A Donegal Trilogy

THE DERRY BOAT

Introduction

Little John Nee

I remember vividly sailing down the Clyde from Glasgow on the Derry boat as a five year old; I remember the cows, I remember the industry of the city, I remember that relatively small ship being tossed around on a stormy sea as she sailed throughout the night to reach Derry in the dawn. Both my parents and my grandparents and most of my extended family had taken that boat in its various incarnations.

 In London in the late seventies while working on the building sites I read Patrick Mc Gill's "Children of the Dead End" and I became inspired; a "navvy" writing the story of his people, my people.

But it was in Marseille in the mid nineties that this show was born. I had spent two months working on a multi-media show, involving the most impressive hydraulic engineering operated through musical instruments connected to the giant computers of the day. But we were slaves to the temperaments of the machine and as I watched the computer doctors scratch their heads I thought "Aren't human beings great bits of stuff?" And we have been for a long time. I decided to tell a story about humans from Donegal.

When I told my good friend Pauric Breathnach my idea for the show he was most encouraging and supportive as he frequently has been down all the years, only more so. His experience, advice, and generosity of spirit were invaluable and there is no doubt but that I couldn't have done it without him.

When I suggested the idea toTraolach O' Fionnain, the County Arts Officer for Donegal, he set about commissioning the show "The Derry Boat" for the Earagail Arts Festival.

Next on board was another good friend Fergal Gallagher an accomplished musician, master carpenter and person you'd want to have beside you if things got difficult. His music inspired and carried the show.

With very little money we began our first weeks rehearsal in the country kitchen of Pauric's rented cottage. There are a couple of items from his kitchen still in the show, as is Fergal Gallagher's tow rope. Pauric had passed some rusty tin at the side of the road and got the idea for the set, Fergal's neighbour had just put a new roof on his barn so he had access to rusty tin, eight pounds cash was spent on some scrap timber and hinges and they built the set on a Saturday. A weeks rehearsal in the Town Hall Studio Galway and a weeks rehearsal in the old Town Hall Ramelton. I do this story no justice by being so brief.

The Derry Boat has since been many places, parish halls and state of the art theatres and thankfully played to mostly full houses. It has been performed on the Isle of Skye and Innisboffin, in Culdaff and Clonakilty, but the highlight so far has been a sell out run in the legendary Citizens Theatre in Glasgow in the heart of the Gorbals; across the road Feda O Donnell's buses still bring people from Glasgow back to Donegal.

The Derry Boat could not have travelled so far without Jim Faulkner who created a lighting design, operated the desk and drove the van. Or without the music of Kevin Duffy who toured with the show, loaded and built the set with me in every venue without a word of complaint. Or without Mike Diskin of the Town Hall Theatre Galway who produced those glorious tours when we three men in a van sailed The Derry Boat.

THE DERRY BOAT

Set in a tin shed in North West Donegal

Time – Present Day

Interior rusty corrugated tin shed; the door is a country half-door. Downstage left there are two barrels ("first barrel" and "mine barrel") There is a small farm stool just inside the door upstage left. Inside the door upstage right there is a wooden chair. Beside it, stage right is a tea chest with a stick, protruding. Above the tea chest a coil of rope is hanging on the wall. Directly downstage of the tea chest there is a wooden box containing cottage props. A watering can sits stage left of this box.

LIGHTS UP ON SHED – CRUNCHY GUITAR CHORD

SECOND GUITAR CHORD – the top half of the door swings open, after a short pause Shughie O'Donnell's head rises from the horizon of the half door.

THIRD GUITAR CHORD – Shughie O'Donnell kicks open the bottom half of the door and enters waving a small pistol around in a gangster pose, he is wearing a crumpled suit, sunglasses, and a porkpie hat.

SHUGHIE The name's O'Donnell, Shughie O'Donnell, Shughie kill or be killed O'Donnell. Last time I was here was with Alison a couple of years back. Over on holidays, out walking the hills and it started to the rain. Came in here for shelter, took off our wet clothes *(smiles remembering)*. This is the site of my ancestral home. Look at it now. It's like a documentary for the National Geographic channel – Lost Kingdom of the Creepie Crawlies.

(Tilts oil barrel and points gun at woodlice)

Freeze Mother Fuckers – legs in the air, everybody legs in the air!

(Addressing a woodlice)

Did you see that? The way yer pals went away and left ye? Ye should listen to your Mammy and stay away fe that crowd.

Relax. I'm no sure how this thing works.

(Crosses to tea-chest and drops the gun in it)

Mind you, there's some people around these parts would say the only good woodlice is a dead woodlice! But not me. Not Cosmic Shughie, the Ghandi of the Gorbals. I used to be a woodlice myself.

(Begins to sing gentle parody of a sean nós)

Come all ye young Woodlice and listen to me
Pay heed to my advice, tis given for free
Don't spend your entire life on your hands and knees
Or dreaming about Woodlice in Los Angeles

And what of the stout lads down on the Antarctic
It's not Guinness nor dominoes that's giving them comfort
When the Huskies are a cowering and an iced wind does blow
Tis thoughts of the homeland melts holes in the snow

Have no fear of trouble, have no fear of travel
And don't be afraid to be vulnerable
'Tis known down the mine shaft, it's known down the tunnels
There is no one so brave as the brave O'Donnells.

(Song ends with Shughie standing front stage right,
his foot on a wooden box)

BLACKOUT

(Spotlight/torchlight on little white Irish cottage on top of a rough brown
door mat placed on top of the box)

Once upon a time a long long time ago in the land of Tir Connell.

(pours water from watering can over the cottage to create rain effect)

LIGHTS UP

There was a lovely wee house, a lovely wee house full of O'Donnells. Wall to wall O'Donnells. More O'Donnells than you could shake a stick at.

The widow O'Donnell and her thirteen assorted O'Donnell children. They lived on a boggy piece of land... *(lifts the cottage with one hand and the doormat with the other allowing water to run off the mat)...* that was worth nothing and cost them everything.

Many's the morning the old widow would say: *(whipping out black headscarf from box and putting it on)*

WIDOW Oh Holy God, what will we eat today? *(sound of knocking)*
I wonder who that could be?

SHUGHIE And the door splintered, boots came flying kicking.

BRITISH CAPTAIN Hello Mrs. O'Donnell – it's us the military.

Please step outside and allow us to knock the stuffing out of you. *(Brief vignette of widow being dragged out by her head)*

It's what we do best. We do it all over the world and we're good at it! My Mrs. O'Donnell, what a lovely home you've got. *(Removes roof from cottage)*

WIDOW *(on her knees with rosary beads)*
What will we do now with no roof over our heads.
Don't talk like that John. No one is leaving this house! No one is leaving this house.

SHUGHIE John O'Donnell, the eldest son, walked down the boreen, towards the station, his head full of notions spinning like a big mill wheel. Sadness and Gladness.

JOHN O'DONNELL *(Singing as he walks)* **Oh then fair thee well sweet Donegal...**

And the sun rose unopposed over Muckish
(Sings) **The Rosses and Gweedore...**
And a fresh fog floated over the bog
(Sings) **It breaks my heart from you to part!**

And the Londonderry and Lough Swilly Locomotive
Swallowed coal and spat steam!
There were wains for the hiring in the Lagan,
tunnel tigers and tatie hokers for Scotland.
Congregating in the station, cramming together,
clambering on the train! Away we go... Gweedore no more.

STATION PORTER All aboard! All aboard the Derry train, serving Creeslough, Kilmacrennan, and Churchill. All aboard, change at Letterkenny for Strabane, All aboard.

(John O Donnell sprints to catch the train, rocks with its motion after boarding)

JOHN O'DONNELL The clattering train with a song of its own and the smoke rising up fluffy black, falling back like a scarf in the wind. And the land being torn backwards. Meenabeg, Meenabawn, the lambs' glen, torn backwards away from our eyes, but stuck forever in our hearts.

And Wee Mary Duffy, wee Mary Duffy with the big red eyes. Sitting wondering "why, why God, why"... *(falls asleep; head is rocked wildly by the loco motion)*

TRAIN WHISTLE

(He is awoke with a jolt as the train stops at a station)

Cashel na gCorr, thon's Gortahork now. Christ that's a sight I'll miss, Tory Island out in the ocean.

OLD MAN WITH BAD LEG Och, away ye go. Don't talk to me about Tory. I am sick of looking at it. Move over and let an old man on the train would ye? Are ye off to Scotland? Scotland is a great country. Plenty of work in Scotland. *(Aside to other passengers)* They would get up and give an old man a seat on a train in Scotland, they would! This country is no bloody good at all. I wouldn't bother coming back at all if it wasn't for the wife and the wains.

(Looking out) Thank God Dunfanaghy Station is nowhere near Dunfanaghy, that's one place I don't like going. I have a sister married in Dunfanaghy. God help the poor cretter who married her! And they say there does be the ghosts of the women and children dead from the workhouse walking the streets...

TRAIN WHISTLE

There's Letterkenny now *(to little boy leaving the train)* there's a farthing for yourself young fella and mind yourself working with them farmers around Letterkenny. They'll have you up in the morning before you're in bed at night, chasing cows and milking pigs.

Stay away from the girls or they'll have you married before you're shaving. Six years of age I was when I went there first. I hadn't a word of English.

They kept me out in the shed with the animals.

TRAIN WHISTLE

That's Derry now wee girl. Out of my way I have a boat to catch. Get the hell out of this country. *(Exits)*

DECKHAND/HARRY DEENEY *(enters)* Where do you think you're going, it's cows first, people after. Ladies and Gentlemen... cows, bullocks, heifers and calves. The Glasgow Steam Company warmly welcomes you aboard the pride of the line for the voyage of a lifetime... on the Derry Boat. Mind your toes – cows coming on.

> **The cows skitter on the Derry Boat**
> **The cows skitter on the Derry Boat**
> **I used to be a stevedore on the Derry Docks**
> **Now I'm like a matador on the Derry Boat**
> **The cows skitter on the Derry Boat**

> **Well the women all pray but the men get drunk**
> **The women all pray while the men get drunk**
> **The Derry Boat, it's a curse**
> **The cows smell bad, but the people smell worse**

(While singing he puts a chair on top of box down stage right and ties a rope to it.)

(Moves centre stage holding rope)

> **Well the cows all sing on the Derry Boat**
> **The cows all sing on the Derry Boat** *(Swings rope like a cows tail)*
> **Mooo, Mooo, the Derry Boat**

(Ties rope to barrel stage left. Rope now stretches across the stage to create deck effect)

All together now, the bit everybody is waiting for – chance of a lifetime. After me everybody...

(Sings) **Moooo** *(Hand to ear prompts audience response)* **Moooo**
Moooo *(Hand to ear prompts audience response)* **Moooo**
Moooo *(Hand to ear prompts audience response)* **Moooo**
Moooo *(Hand to ear prompts audience response)* **Moooo**
Moooo *(Hand to ear prompts audience response)* **Moooo**
The Derry Boat!

God, you people have no shame whatsoever.
(Musical accompaniment becomes fast and frantic)

(Harry Deeney is flung from one side of the deck to the other, clings to deck rope, threatening sea sickness)

The sea gets rough, cows get sick
The sea gets rough, cows get sick
The sea gets rough, cows get sick
A Navvy gets drunk and I get hit!
The Derry boat.

Slow down young fella. We're not going to get there any faster, you playing at that speed. *(Music stops)* Must have a girlfriend waiting for him in Glasgow. Unfortunate woman. *(Crosses stage holding on to deck rope)* God she's choppy the night boys *(sits on top of barrel looks out to sea – fog horn)*

Join the Merchant Navy. See the world. Sail away out of Derry… all the way to Glasgow. Then back to Derry. Then back to Glasgow. Derry, Glasgow, Glasgow Derry.

Meet interesting people… from Donegal.

Learn things you never knew… about cows.

See yonder Inishowen – they are all out with the tablecloths and bedsheets, waving them like flags, saying goodbye to the ones they love the most. *(Turns to look at the people behind him on the deck)* God, how could anybody love them cretturs. And the old women praying like mad. They reckon St. Colmcille prophesised that the Derry Boat would never sink. Easy knowing he never travelled with the Glasgow Steam Ship Company; for the only thing keeping this tub afloat is the fact that she leaks out water faster than she lets it in.

But I don't care. I'll be out of here in a couple of weeks. Starting a new job.

Sailing out of Belfast on a luxury cruise liner, The White Star Line, across the Atlantic Ocean. Might meet myself some rich ould yankie doll. Get married and come back to Derry a rich man! You'll see me dandering down Ship Quay Street with a dickie-bow on me. Able bodied sea-man first class Harry Deeny the S.S. Titanic.

My luck is starting to look up. *(Begins scratching all over)* I've been hanging around with Donegal people too long.

JOHN O'DONNELL *(leaning on the chair at other end of rope creating a rocking effect)*

And in the morning the Clyde; green at the cuffs; wide and welcoming, Greenock and Gouroch, up past the tug boats and coal barges. Ferries full of workers and big ships the size of a small farm of land. On either side there's green fields, big fields, the greenest fields you have ever seen in your life. What you might call Protestant-looking fields. Up towards the Broomielaw, up past the industrial spew where the sewers start spitting in. Where holy Saint Mungo caught the holy salmon saying "Let Glasgow Flourish" – well here she is now: Flourishing shipbuilding, Flourishing Steel-works, Flourishing munitions factories, Flourishing fat landlords – Let Glasgow Flourish! *(Unties rope)*

(Uses rope as a hammer, striking between lines)

The anvil of the Empire, Sledgehammer of the Sovereign. Big smelly, sweaty, sooty and socialist.

(Pulls stick from tea-chest to reveal a red flag, waves it in iconic Red Clydesider pose)

(Sings) **Then Raise the scarlet standard high**
Beneath its shade we live or die
When cowards flinch and traitors sneer
We'll keep the red flag flying here.

(Flings flag)

Glasgow and John O'Donnell came face to face, stripped to the waist and embraced

(Grabs chair and swings it back)

GANGERMAN Come on Donegal get your back into it!

> (John O'Donnell labours, pulling the rope and coiling it, tossing it. Swings
> the barrel onto his shoulder, plodding through mud, swings it down behind
> the wooden box stage right. Turns and pulls 3x2 timber from mine-barrel
> and swings it like a sledge hammer onto first barrel, then swings it like
> a hammer onto mine barrel again onto first barrel and again onto mine
> barrel; creating flowing images of industrial labour.)

JOHN O'DONNELL *(leaning on 3x2 timber)* The Gorbals was alive with poor
people, Jewish refugees from Eastern Europe, poor Catholics from the West
of Ireland, A wheena wee Presbyterians from the Highlands and Islands
and plenty of good-hearted heathens from Glasgow.

> *(Lifts tea chest and places down stage left and sits on it)*

Our people were gathered from one end of the Gorbals to the other.
Cumbernauld Street in those days was hummin' with the smell of ripe
horse dung. It was a great time for horses. There were plenty of them.
They had a good social life. Mind you, when the wind blew over from the
knackers yard, they'd get that worried look on their faces and the heads
would go down into the nose bags, pretending it wasn't happening. They
were a lot like our own people.

I remember Mickey Bradley's first day in Glasgow he says to me:

MICKEY God John a Donnell aren't the Glasgow people very mean all the
same and they wouldn't spend a wheena shillings on white-wash for them
dirty buildings over there!

JOHN O'DONNELL God Mickey, you knew nothing then and you know
nothing now. Everywhere in Glasgow was black with ould industrial soot
do you see? For every drop of rain that fell in Glasgow was thick with soot.
There was washing hanging everywhere, everywhere that washing could
hang, there was washing hanging, ould worn white sheets and the rain
would come down and leave big black streaks down the sheets.

Wee Mary Duffy from our place. She was working with old Rosie helping
her to keep lodgers. Sewing, mending, cooking, anything needed done
she do it.

When the rain would come she'd panic and go running down the stairs three at a time out into the backyard to try to save the sheets from the soot, she'd gather them all up and bring them out of the rain. Trailing them through the mud!

Ah but she was a hard worker. Mind you, she would go to a dance when she got a chance, and I'd give her a dance when I got the chance and I made sure I got the chance!

"SHOE THE DONKEY" TUNE
(John O Donnell approaches Mary)

Mary, God, Mary, Glasgow agrees with you. You get more and more beautiful every time I see you. I think I'll have to stop seeing you for you're getting that good looking you're starting to hurt my eyes.

(Comic clumsy dance leading to close dance and embarrassment at arousal)

God Mary, you're a great dancer all the same. Do you know what I was thinking Mary? Maybe after work in the evenings I could call around to you and you could teach me a few steps… stop blushing Mary. You are aye blushing and the whole hall looking at you.

The happiest days of my life were spent making that woman blush. After the dance we'd walk down South Portland Street together, arm in arm, talking about Donegal and all the old friends we used to have and the games we would play in the Summer's evening. *(Lifts a horse shoe and mimics play and drops it in tea chest).* Then we would start to talk about how fond of each other we were and how could two people as fond of each other as we were of each other possibly get more fond of each other. Well I had one idea and she had a totally different idea. The talk soon got around to marriage. Talk like that, a man would want to be making good money. So I got a new job going down holes looking for coal.

BLACKOUT

(Mine-barrel placed in position on top of tea chest. LX Light goes down barrel creating tunnel)

(Sings) **"In the corner of the Glen there's a gang of Mountain Men would gather in the evenings throwing horseshoes"**

Are you there Mickey? (*Looks back down the tunnel*) You'd be glad of a day in the bog after this. Mickey, when I decided to come to Scotland I had no idea it was the bottom half I'd be looking at. Never mind, we'll go back to Ireland rich men and buy a pub each, one on either side of the street and we'll give away the drink for free! God but they'll be glad to see us. Mickey.

BLACKOUT

(*Tilts barrel vertical still resting on tea chest. Lights up on pithead. John appears up the barrel from mine shaft*).

Saturday then was the day off work. We'd go and watch Celtic play football. There's a fella plays for them named Patsy Gallagher from Ramelton, maybe you know him? God I thought everyone knew Patsy. Anyway they can't stop him scoring goals. It's hard to beat a Donegal man.

Sundays we would go down to Saint Francis to mass. After mass, Mary and me might take a wee walk. But that's our business and not yours. Monday morning back down the bloody hole.

BLACKOUT

(*Tilts mine barrel back into tunnel position on top of tea chest. LX Light goes down barrel creating tunnel*)

(*Looking behind him into the tunnel*) What are you saying? God Mickey, you don't miss a trick! (*Facing forward*) There's nothing that you don't know about. And if you don't know about it, you want to know about it. That is correct. I was not at Celtic on Saturday. You should start up one of those Pinkerton Detective Agencies. I will tell you where I was. Myself and Mary went down to St. Francis' and were married at three o clock on Saturday. Thank you. Then we went up to Paddy's Market and bought a pair of curtains. Us didn't have a room to put them up in, but Old Rosie sorted us out wi' a single end room and she gave us two cups as a wedding present. She says if she is going to come and visit us she will bring another cup for herself. God it's good to have something to look forward to in the evenings Mickey.

BLACKOUT

(*Tilts barrel vertical still resting on tea chest. Lights up on pithead. John appears up the barrel from mine shaft*).

Well you should have kept your bloody head out of the way! They say there is nothing as dangerous as a happy man – well, there is – a happy man swinging a pick and there's none more dangerous than me for there's none more happy than me. I swear to God when I go down that road in the evenings, the young fellas all do be laughing at me. Me skipping along the road like a young lamb, back to them dirty old tenements but sure what do I care. My feet hardly touch the stairs. I float right up them and into the front room and there she is, the most beautiful picture in all God's creation – my darling wee baby daughter Annie and her smiling up at me with a big stupid smile and me smiling back at her with a big stupid smile. A man wouldn't have to eat or sleep or drink or do anything at all only to look at you all day and all night. Aren't you beautiful? You have got your daddy's good looks. We called her Annie after me own mother. We reckon if we put by wheena shillings this year we'll go back to Donegal and let the two of them meet up. Mind you there's no money made on these streets smiling at babies. Any money made around here is made down the big bloody hole.

BLACKOUT

(*Tilts mine barrel back into tunnel position on top of tea chest. LX Light goes down barrel creating tunnel*)

Coughs – Mickey I was wondering – all this overtime we're getting because of the war, will the Germans be getting that overtime too? Are there hundreds of wee German miners down under the ground digging like mad now? Jesus Mickey, we might bump into them. Oh I'm not complaining. I'm glad of every penny and every farthing that I get. When this one's born that'll be three. Well there's Annie, there's Michael and we reckon if this one's a good-looking boy, we'll call him John after me. God, but there's great breeding stock in the O'Donnells.

BLACKOUT

(*Tilts barrel vertical still resting on tea chest. Lights up on pithead. John appears up the barrel from mine shaft*).

If Mickey hadn't pulled me out of the way I would have stayed stood where I was standing and let that coal cart come and cut me in half. For I would be a better off lying dead down there than having to climb up here to this awful bloody world.

To drag my feet down thon dirty old road back to them dirty old rotten tenements. To drag my feet up them stairs and before I even go into the house I know I'll hear the baby crying, looking for attention, getting none. And when I go in the door wee Michael will be looking up at me and him trying to mind the baby all on his own, looking up at me for answers. God son I have no answers. And Mary'll be sitting there looking into the Fireplace, no fire lit. God knows what's going on in her head for she hasn't spoken to anyone for two weeks now. It breaks my heart to look at her. And I can't even close my eyes at night. For every time I close my eyes I see the face of my own wee darlin Annie and her lying in the wee coffin, dead of consumption. Never caused no harm to nobody. She brought nothing to this world only happiness and I had to stand and watch them put the wee box into the dirt and all I wanted to do was to climb down beside her and hold her, hold the wee box close to me for I will never see her again, never see her again.

And Father Gallagher turned around to my Mary at the graveside and said that it was God's will that she died. If I had heard him I would have choked him for curse you Father Gallagher, curse you and curse your bloody useless God.

BLACKOUT

(Tilts mine barrel back into tunnel position on top of tea chest. LX Light goes down barrel creating tunnel)

(Coughing and choking on dust) God Mickey –do you not think that we'll be under the ground long enough when we are dead. What are we doing here now?

There's boys that's not dead a fortnight, if they had the same choice as us – they would scratch their way to the top and they wouldn't even look down to tie their shoelaces. Mickey – I need fresh air, I need fresh air. (Screams) I need fresh air.

BLACKOUT

(Swings barrel off tea chest)

SHUGHIE I think Granda thought he was going to get a wee holiday when he joined the British Army. So he did! Two lovely weeks in the North of France throwing horse shoes with his pals. He sent my Granny a postcard "wish you were here" then he got sent down the trenches and got gassed, got his right arm blown off him. Poor granny was left down the Gorbals wi' two hungry wains hanging off her and no money. On Saturday she used to go up to Glasgow Green to hear big Alan Campbell speak: *(Knocks down wooden box stage right to use as soap box)*

ALAN CAMPBELL Brothers and Sisters, I just came doon fe Queen Street Station and I just saw a picture of a man on the wall. A man by the name of Kitchener, you know who I'm talking about, Mr. Pointy Finger. "Your Country Needs You". Aye, your country hen. That's the country that I'm talking about. The country that has you in a wee house with the rain coming through the roof and the wind blowing right through it. Your wains are oot the back playing with rats and it's a sad day when you can look at a rat and know it's better fed than your own children. Everyday your men folk are going away, to fight in the fields of France, your husbands, your brothers, your fathers and your sons. And there's many that won't come back again. A couple of years down the road, The King of England and the Kaiser of Germany'll be sitting together having a wee glass of brandy for those boys are related you know? "No hard feelings old chap!"

But we'll no' get to meet the German workers, we will not, for if we did we might find out that we have a lot in common with them – we have a common enemy. For our enemy is not the worker of another country, our enemy is poverty, our enemy is hunger, our enemy is ignorance. A mighty enemy and it'll take a mighty army to defeat it, but we have the mightiest army in the whole world. The workingman and the workingwoman standing together, shoulder-to-shoulder, arm in arm, united. As my friend James Connolly always says "We serve neither King nor Kaiser". *(Strikes iconic labour leader pose)*.

SHUGHIE *(Sits on box)* They used to take being poor very seriously in them days. It's no' that long since I was poor myself you know, but that's all in the past. *(Fetches suitcase)* My babies will want for nothing, my babies; Alison's babies, well they're mine too. They are not even born yet, she's not even pregnant, she's not even trying! She should have been here ages ago *(Goes to door and looks out down the hill)* I spend half my life waiting for her. If she had a phone I'd call her. *(Mimics Alison)* "I'm no' going to get one o' they things. They're radioactive. Fry my brain. I'll end up like you." I'll phone her mother – she always knows what's happening *(Produces mobile phone. Keys in number)*. No Bloody coverage. *(Moves around trying to get a signal. Ends up on standing on top of first barrel)* Ah come on, my battery's low, hurry up.

(Mimicking Alison's mother) "Hello this is Mandy McKay, I'm no' in. I must be oot. Leave a wee message and I'll get back to you".

Hello Mrs. McKay – this is Shughie. I'm waiting for Alison in Donegal. If she contacts you will you tell her to contact me? Byeee. *(Puts phone away. Jumps off barrel.)* Bitch. She is. She's a toxic bitch. See that. I'm uptight just talking to her answering machine. I know what's going to happen. Alison will walk in that door.

Where the hell were you?

None of your bloody business that's where!

Chill out Shughie. Breathe. I am at peace.

(Imagines Alison arriving) Is that you hen? Oh Aye, I was just doing a wee bit of meditation. I was thinking about all the money I am going to spend on you. First thing in the morning I'm going to buy a new car, one of them American jobs with fins up the back.

> *(Sings)* **Saw you standing in Sauchihall Street,**
> **platform shoes and dungarees**
> **I didn't mind that you were taller than me,**
> **see I could see you had pedigree**
> **I wished that I had money so I could say let's go away**
> **but because I hadn't got any I put it off for another day. Yeah!**
>
> **You and me and a full tank of petrol**
> **You and me and a full tank of petrol**
> **You and me and a full tank of petrol**
>
> **Hot wired a Mercedes that Friday night**
> **Ran red lights like a Jacobite**
> **I hit the brakes and you walked into sight**
> **Said You and me baby we are like meteorites**
>
> **Hand break turns on the urban waste ground**
> **'till that car would go no more.**
> **We held hands and watched it burning;**
> **the stars did smile and the moon did roar. Yeah!**

You and me and a full tank of petrol
You and me and a full tank of petrol
You and me and a full tank of petrol

One week it was on the next it was off
But the years went by, we grew soft.
The one thing I could never understand
how come nothing works out the way I planned
But this time it's different 'cos I got the money,
ah honey honey, honey. I got the money.

I can walk into any bar,
Say that's my woman and that's my car
Baby, baby, we'll go far.
Falcarragh to Ardara
'cos I've got a full tank of petrol for you,
I've got a full tank, a full tank, a full tank of petrol for you.

(Shughie gets lost in the song, throwing shapes)

Yeah! Yeah! Yeah! Uhuh, uhuh, uhuh.

(Music stops; Shughie continues. Realising he looks foolish he gives the musician a dirty look)

I come from a long line of good singers. My father Jimmy O'Donnell, singer and fighter.

JIMMY Come on in boys, this is my house, you'se are my friends, come on, on in. Look at the state of this place. Do I have to tidy this house myself? I have to do everything around here myself. Come on in Jock, sit down there, the best seat in the house for the best man in the house, my pal Jock. This is my father and this is my missus, no bloody wonder I have to go to the pub every night, looking at your miserable faces? Cheer up would you. You do have a choice hen, this is your choice here. *(Shows fist)* Come on in Charlie, sit down there pal. You know my father don't you Charlie? Lost his arm fighting in the war. Whose side were you on Da? Ha ha ha. He doesn't like it when I say that. Relax would ye. Sing a wee song Jock, have a wee drink. *(Hands cup to Jock. Jock drinks He is very drunk).*

JOCK   **The Northern Lights of Aberdeen**
        Is home sweet home to me
        The Northern Lights of Aberdeen
        Is where I long to be

JIMMY   Aye, lovely stuff Jock. Here Charlie, sing an Irish song and shut that
        Scotch cunt up!

CHARLIE *(Stands up, staggering and sings)*

        Three leafed shamrock I adore thee
        Your three leafs I long to see
        When there's better days in Ireland
        I'll come home and marry thee.

JIMMY   Lovely stuff Charlie. I'm surprised you huvnae won any prizes for your
        singing. I'll sing a wee song myself if naebody has any objections to me
        singing a bloody song in my own bloody house, sing a proper bloody song.

        *(Begins to sing, fists clenched, flashing the occasional menacing glance
        around the room)*

        In Mountjoy Jail one Monday morning,
        high above the gallows tree,
        Kevin Barry gave his young life for the cause of liberty
        Just a lad of eighteen summers,
        yet nobody can deny as he went to death
        that morning proud he held his head up high

        (Jimmy starts to cry...)

        That's all he was Charlie, eighteen years of age. He was only a child. Naebody
        cares about poor Kevin Barry. He died for Ireland. *(Turns to Jock)* You Black
        and Tan bastard. *(Swings and punches him)*

SHUGHIE Aye, that's my father, a sensitive soul. Bare fist fighter all around
        Glasgow. Champion. But he never sold out. Any money he made fighting, he
        spent it on drink.

JIMMY   Come here to me son. I'm not going to hit you. I'm your daddy. I love
        you. *(Reaches and slaps Shughie)* Next time I tell you to come here you come
        here OK? Your nose is getting very big, did you know that? Know what's
        going to happen to you? Some big hun is going to walk down that road

some day and hit you a slap and break your nose. And it'll hurt. Let me do it now and I'll be gentle. Stop whinging, I was only joking. You're like a wee girl. I'm going to go down Paddy's Market and buy you a wee dress. You'll bloody wear it if I tell you to wear it. Ye wee sissy. Go you and get Cassius Clay to hit me then. Cassius Clay is a bloody sissy too. Anyone who wears boxing gloves is a sissy.

SHUGHIE My Da never wore boxing gloves. He couldn't find a pair to fit him. He had hands like the Frankenstein monster. He didn't need them. Particularly when he was hitting wee Katie Dillon. Wee Katie Dillon from the County Mayo. My Mammy. She never once had the indignity of feeling a boxing glove off the side of her head. It was all bare fist in our house. No bloody sissies.

> *(Sings)* **She stands sore looking out the window,**
> **He sits shamed looking into the fire**
> **In a tenement house in Glasgow**
> **Far from here is her hearts desire**
>
> **I don't care about the punches and bruises**
> **I don't care about the pain**
> **I don't care about the greyhounds and horses**
> **I just care about they wains**
>
> **You're a hard man, a scrapper and bruiser**
> **You're telling me it's you wears the trousers**
> **You spend the bru down in the boozer,**
> **You bet the rent on a track full of losers**
>
> **I don't care about the punches and bruises**
> **I don't care about the pain**
> **I don't care about the greyhounds and horses**
> **I just care about they wains**
>
> **Oh Mayo, we're often hungry,**
> **There's no one here to interfere**
> **Virgin Mary mind my babies,**
> **Hear my prayer, hear my prayer,**
> **hear my prayer, Poison his beer**

I can't remember my mammy. She died of TB when I was three. I remember one time she took me and my bother Shamie on the Derry Boat to Donegal, but I can't remember it. I remember every other Summer after that. Down at the Gorbals Cross on a Glasgow fair Saturday. Dozens of Donegal people cramming into these wee vans to take them back to Donegal. Big fat Mas and screaming wains. And their necks would be scrubbed that clean they would be bleeding. And my Da would be off the booze wearing a suit, being polite to everyone.

JIMMY Let me help you with that hen – it's nice to be nice.

SHUGHIE And the wee "commer" vans would be packed that tight the arse would be scraping off the road making sparks. Down to Ardrossan for the crossing and on to the ferry. Straight away I'm up on the deck throwing crisps to the seagulls.

WEE BOY Here boys look at that, look at that. See that, see that big stone sticking out of the water, that big stone sticking out of the water, that's Paddy's milestone, that big stone sticking out of the water.

OTHER WEE BOY You think you know everything, don't you?

SHUGHIE Driving off the ferry into Belfast.

ANOTHER WEE BOY Look at the B Specials.

WEE BOY Don't look at them they'll shoot ye.

SHUGHIE Driving through Northern Ireland. By this stage everybody's getting tired and whingy.

BIG BROTHER Are we nearly there yet Daddy?

WEE SISTER Mammy, when are we going to be there?

YOUNGEST I want to go home.

SHUGHIE And the vans would fill up with cigarette smoke. The smell of baby sick... and dirty nappies, and just when you thought you couldn't take any more we'd cross the border into magic Donegal, a fortnight of heaven just beginning and everyone would smile automatic.

DADDY We are nearly there now son, it won't be long now.

WEE BOY (*frightened*) Daddy what's that over there?

DADDY That's a cow son.

SHUGHIE The cousins would come and meet us off the bus. They were happy
to see us. They weren't just pretending, they really were happy to see us.
They'd take us out to the wee house out in the country... the smell of fresh
cut hay and the smell of fresh baked bread. And the dog would jump up
and lick my face. Get down! The wee house with the nice wallpaper...
and the cups with saucers... and everybody smiling and laughing making
jokes... the nice table cloth... and the Swiss roll.

And I'd a wee room all to myself with blue roses on the wallpaper. And
clean sheets on the bed. I nearly exploded my lungs inhaling them sheets.
I was that tired I couldn't stay awake and that excited I couldn't go to
sleep. (*Mimics young Shughie struggling to stay awake. Then closes eyes.*) And I
dreamed the sweetest dreams I ever dreamt. I woke up in the morning and
I was frightened to open my eyes in case the whole thing was a dream, but
then I smelt the clean sheets and I knew we weren't in our house. I'd jump
out of bed and go running into the kitchen for a big bowl of porridge and I
hated porridge. Except when I was in Donegal. Then, I loved it.

I'd go running out of the house for a day full of fields and I'd shout out loud
from my invisible horse, Silver! He lived in Donegal and he missed me
while I was away. (*Mimes riding invisible horse*) Me and him would mosey on
down to the chaparral to check out Uncle Joe's steers. Keep an eye out for
Apaches 'cos Donegal's crawling with them. And the day I saw the baby fox
up in the meadow and waited all day to see would he come back again, but
he never did. And I missed my tea.

Mostly you would find me down in the wee river. (*Takes off shoes and rolls
up trousers*) The wee Brown burn, up to my knees in water. I practically
lived there. One time, it must have been harvest time 'cos everybody was
out in the fields working and they went for their dinner and I sneaked up
and stole a hay fork and brought it back down to the river to harpoon a
trout. Playing Moby Dick and I slipped on a greasy stone and fell on my
arse in the water and got soaked to the skin. But nobody was angry, they
just all laughed.

UNCLE DANNY "Did ye see what happened to the young fella, he fell in
the water"

SHUGHIE And they told everybody about it. My uncle Danny stopped a
passing tractor

UNCLE DANNY *(Leaning on tractor)* "Here Willie John. Did ye hear what
happened the young fella over from Scotland? He fell in the water. That's a
great young fella. Come over here son. There's nothing he can't do *(rubbing
young Shughie's head)*. He can read the newspaper and everything. He fell in
the water"

SHUGHIE They talked and they talked about it and they told the whole of
Donegal. And after the holidays my wee brother Shamie went and told the
whole of Scotland. Maybe you heard about it, the time I fell in the water?
In the evenings they ducked down their heads and pulled out the Rosary
beads and I'd duck out the back door and duck through the hole in
the hedge and chase the ducks up the road. And the red sky at night, a
shepherd's delight. I'd go up the hill, up to mad Mrs. Gillespie's house.
Everybody said she was a witch, but I liked her. Me and her would go
walking down the wee lane, hand in hand, with a packet of salt, pouring it
on the slugs and watching them melt. *(Smiles mischievously at Mrs Gillespie
and pours salt on the slugs/his shoes)* Then the Summer was over. Back to
Glasgow and my Da would go back on the booze.

You couldn't mention Donegal to Granda, it's all the Promised Land with
him. He never left the house, just sat there reading the bible with his one
good hand.

GRANDA O Lord a God when will we see the Promised Land.

SHUGHIE I remember one time, I was about eight years old, I was lying in
bed, I couldn't sleep, it was about two in the morning. I was looking at
the ceiling and the damp patches and the pictures that they make. I heard
noises in the other room. My brother Shamie was sleeping and my Da was
out boozing. It must be Granda. Granda used to get up in the middle of the
night and pish in the wardrobe. But this time it was different.

I heard him rattle at the door to our room. He came into the room. I closed
my eyes and pretended to be asleep. I sneaked a wee look. He was wearing
his hat and coat. He walked across the room. I knew he was standing right
above me. Dear God, please don't let Granda pish on top of me. He started
to shake me.

GRANDA Shughie, Shughie, get up son. Hurry up and put your clothes on. *(Hands shoe to Shughie)* Quick put on your shoes. You'll have to hurry up now.

SHUGHIE *(Rubbing sleepy eyes)* What is it Grandad, is the house on fire?

GRANDA No Shughie, we're going to the Promised Land.

SHUGHIE *(In disbelief)* Where are we going Granda?

GRANDA The Promised Land.

SHUGHIE *(Putting on shoes)* Granda's finally gone chop suey. They're going to stick him in the mental hospital and we'll have to go and visit him on Sundays. That means I won't be able to play football on Sundays all because of him. He took me by the hand and took me down the stairs and out into the street. The rain had just stopped and the streets were all black and shiny. I looked up at my Granda, he was smiling. I never seen him smiling before, I never seen him out of the house before.

SHUGHIE Granda where did you say we were going?

GRANDA We're going to the Promised Land. We're going to paradise.

SHUGHIE Are we going to Parkhead Granda?

GRANDA No' that paradise, the other one.

SHUGHIE We walked down Crown Street. Up ahead I spotted a polis man standing at the traffic lights. "Oh oh now we're in trouble". I looked down at my Granda's feet, he was wearing his carpet slippers, he used to call them his "holy slippers" because they were full of holes. All he had on underneath his overcoat was his dirty long-johns, you could see the white skin on his chest; if you didn't know him he'd frighten ye. We're going to get lifted. We're going to go to jail. I don't want to go to jail. But Granda just walked right up to the polis man and said "Good evening officer, it's a lovely evening for an old veteran to be out walking" and the polis man just saluted at him.

SHUGHIE I forgot Granda. You are a war hero. Aren't you Granda? You should have stayed in the army Granda, see if you'd a stayed in the army you'd a been a general by now. Wouldn't ye Granda? Granda can I look in the toy shop window? Can I Granda, please Granda, just a wee minute? Can I?

GRANDA No Shughie we have no time to be looking in toyshop windows. You can get all the toys you want in the Promised Land if you hurry up.

SHUGHIE What else can you get in the Promised Land Granda?

GRANDA You can get anything you want if you hurry up.

SHUGHIE Granda can I get a dog?

GRANDA Aye, ye can get a dog.

SHUGHIE Well, why didn't you not tell me about this before Granda? Come on. Hurry up... I looked up at the sky and the clouds were all blue in the moonlight and they were like huge sailing ships and they were all sailing in the one direction. The same direction as us, towards the Promised Land. On either side of the street stood a line of lamp-posts, tall and proud and at the top of every lamp post sat a huge golden angel saying "this way to the promised land, this way to the promised land".

Granda, I'm hungry. Will we be able to get anything to eat when we get to the Promised Land?

GRANDA You'll be able to get anything you want to eat in the Promised Land.

SHUGHIE But Granda, will they not all be sleeping?

GRANDA Shughie, yer mammy'll be waiting for you, she'll have the dinner on.

SHUGHIE But my mammy's not in the Promised Land, my mammy's in the graveyard. Then I saw the toyshop window. Stop Granda! We're not going to the Promised Land! We're walking around The Gorbals in circles. Stop Granda, stop!

GRANDA (Stops. Looks bewildered. Clutching the place where his arm used to be) I want to go home, (Confused, begins to weep) I want to go home, I want to go home.

SHUGHIE (Reaching for Granda's hand and leading him) Come on Granda, I'll take you home.

And I made up my mind that when I grew up I'd play for Glasgow Celtic and get to be a rich man.

And I'd bring Granda back to Donegal and tell him it was The Promised Land…

Mind the dog shite Granda!.

Now he's dead and I'm a rich man. Typical, he couldn't wait.

GRANDA Oh, I'm going to die a poor man.

SHUGHIE Well you did, I hope you're happy.

See if I'd have lived in America, I could have sued him and my father for the amount of negativity they kept in the house. It is a miracle I'm not damaged. But Alison sorted me out with the affirmations. You know affirmations, it's like (struggles to articulate)… it's like… you can get books about it.

Yesterday morning I slept in. I was late for Yoga. I don't particularly want to go to Yoga, but Alison wants me to go to Yoga so I go to Yoga. I go out the door, press the lift button, the lift is broken surprise surprise. Walk down thirteen flights of pishy stairs and out into the pishy rain. In my pocket twenty pounds for Yoga and I've no' got the bus fair – be positive. The rain is refreshing me. The rain is refreshing me. I am enlivened by the heavenly showers. Every single drop of rain that falls on me, sets me free and a step closer to enlightenment. I'm fucking singing in the rain. I was just getting into it when the rain stopped. Stick with it Shughie You're on a roll. I am prosperous, I am prosperous. Prosperity is just around the corner, pros…. per….ity is just a…round the corner, then bang, prosperity my arse. It's old Willie Doherty the wino.

WILLIE (Inebriated; grabs and clutches Shughie's hand) Hi Shughie son, I knew your Granda well.

SHUGHIE Aye Willie, ah know. Here Willie give me back my hand. I need it. I know it doesn't mean much to you Willie, but I'm late for yoga. I pulled my hand free, he staggered backwards. He slipped. He fell. He banged his head on the wall. Split it open. There was blood everywhere. Ah Jesus. I went into Silver's bookie shop. Here Bilko, phone an ambulance quick. It's an emergency it doesn't cost anything. Came out of the bookies shop. There were these two biddies standing there.

1ST BIDDY Is he deed?

2ND BIDDY No loss if he was, dirty old wino.

SHUGHIE Ladies, please, that's a human being you're talking about... Bilko comes out of the bookie shop

BILKO Here Hughie, do you want to do a wee job for me?

SHUGHIE I'm busy here Bilko.

BILKO What's the matter? My money no good enough for you?

SHUGHIE The ambulance comes. We put him into the ambulance. (*To ambulance medics*) How should I know where he lives. (*Aside to Bilko*) He's homeless. (*Back to medics*) See they luxury apartments over there? I think he lives in one of them. He's an eccentric. Make sure you look after him.

BILKO Do you want to do a job for me or not?

SHUGHIE Aye, a'right Bilko.

He throws me the car keys and we get into the car. It was a nice motor. One of they classic jobs. A tap on the window.

1ST BIDDY Excuse me son, yer pal forgot his plastic bag.

SHUGHIE (*Mimes taking the plastic bag*) Aye, well he isn't my pal. Where are we going Bilko?

BILKO Shut up and drive.

SHUGHIE How can I drive when I don't know where we are going?

BILKO Drive.

SHUGHIE Where are we going? The Three Hens? The Three Hens in Ibrox? You're mental. I'm not getting out of the car. I don't care how much money you give me, I'm not getting out of the car. That was a long time ago. I used to be mental, but you're mental all by yourself today.

Pull up outside the Three Hens in Ibrox. He goes in and I pick up the Mobily phone.

SHUGHIE Hello enquiries? Could you connect me with the Vickie hospital. *(Speaking posh Glasgow)* Hello, is that the Victoria Infirmary? I'm making an enquiry about a gentleman who was admitted this morning, a Mister William Doherty. *(Listens and responds in his own accent)* Aye the wino. He's dead? Willie Doherty's dead.

The car door opens and Bilko gets in. He throws something, I catch it. It's a gun. My brain goes all Sesame Street on me. The gun's hot. How got the gun hot? The gun got hot cause the gun got shot.

BILKO Are you on drugs or something. Get out of here fast.

SHUGHIE I pull out, I nearly get sandwiched between two buses. I'm trying to get my head together, trying to think of the appropriate affirmation, but my brain's stuck in Sesame Street. The gun is hot. How got the gun hot? The gun got hot cause the gun got shot.

BILKO Shughie, pull up over there. Put that gun in your pocket.

We are in big trouble. You're the one with the gun in your pocket. You're going to have to get rid of it. Throw it in the river. Don't worry about it. That river's full of guns, and here, take this with ye and bring it to my shop just after six a clock tonight *(Handing suitcase to Shughie)*. And don't even think about getting out of this car without taking that wino's plastic bag with you.

SHUGHIE He drives off, leaves me standing at the side of the road in the pishing rain. In my pocket a lethal weapon, possibly evidence in a homicide, a mysterious suitcase and a dead man's plastic bag. It was hard to be positive. I stepped in to the park to shelter beneath a tree. I spotted a bin. I was about to throw the plastic bag into the bin when it occurred to me "this is all he had to show for a lifetime's labour" labour exchange actually. Then I remembered. There was a story he had a sister living in the posh part of town, always trying to sort him out. I might do a wee bit of detective work and track her down.

Ding Dong "Excuse me hen, I was with your brother when he passed away. He was very fond of you. Your name was the last words on his lips. I know it's not much but he wanted you to have this plastic bag."

Och it cheered me up thinking about it. Then I went into the Natural History Museum, cheers me up looking at stuffed squirrels too. I put down the suitcase, I turn around and the suitcase is gone. The security man has it. Excuse me mister that's my suitcase. Aye, well it's not a bomb is it? *(Suddenly realising it may very well be a bomb for all he knows Shughie holds the suitcase very sheepishly)*

I walk down the steps very very carefully and then I ran all the way to Bilko's. I got around the corner to Bilko's street and there was a crowd of people, two polis cars and that plastic "scene of the crime" tape around the bookies.

(To woman) Excuse me hen, what happened here? Mr. Silver's dead? Poor old Bilko eh? *(In shock)* He was an awfully nice man...

I turned around the corner and I ran. I ran all the way to Alison's block. The lift always works in her block. It must be the affirmations. I ring the doorbell and there she is, the love of my life. Kiss, kiss, kiss.

I have to go to the toilet. I love you. *(Throws suitcase on top of barrel as if to open it but doesn't – describing it instead)* When I opened it up I was hit with the smell of money. My money. Dirty used banknotes. I'm prosperous. I really fucking am prosperous. Here Alison, look at that *(holding up imaginary wad of notes)*. It's money, it's my money. I mean it's our money, we're rich. What do you mean "how did I get it?" Affirmations. Trust me alright. You're the one that's always going on about trust in a relationship. Look all you have to do is first thing in the morning get on Feda O'Donnell's bus, you're going to Donegal. I'll be there waiting for you. You just get on the bus, get off the bus at Letterkenny. *(Responding to her reaction)* I'm no' asking you to live there just get off the bus there. Go into Boyce's café, check to see if anybody is following you. I don't know why I said that...it's got nothing to do with the money... it's because you're an attractive woman... somebody might be following you. Do what you want to do. Get a taxi past Falcarragh, past Gortahork, swing a second left up that wee road, past Sweeney's B&B. Do you remember we stayed there on holidays? Remember Mrs. Sweeney with the varicose veins and you told her at breakfast that acupuncture would cure her varicose veins? Aye that Mrs. Sweeney. Remember the wee tin shed up on the hill? Remember I told you my Grandfather was born there? Remember it was raining? *(Softly)* Remember Alison, we took off our clothes? *(Annoyed because she doesn't remember)* Remember Alison, remember? *(She remembers-she's been winding him up)* I knew you remembered. Stop doing that. It's not funny. Undermining my self-confidence. Anyway, I'll be waiting for you in the wee tin shed. I'll explain everything then.

> *(He turns to get ready to go, then responding to Alison telling him his father has been looking for him, he turns back)*

What time was that at? Did he say what he wanted? Probably looking for drink money. I better check.

(To audience) My da was looking for me.

Here, keep an eye on that for me *(Hands her the suitcase)*. See that plastic bag, throw it in the bin, belonged to a wino. Down the pub. My father practically lives there. Here Da, can't dally, there's a ton, have a drink on me. He didn't even say thank you. I hope he drinks himself to death. Step outside the pub, two dodgy geezers sitting in a red BMW, broken noses, scars on their faces. Stereotypical thugs. I didn't want to rush to form a judgement, but I start walking faster. They get out of the car and start to follow me. I walk faster, they walk faster. I duck down a lane, they are right behind me. I start to run. They run after me, I jump over the fence into the park, they're right behind me. Get to Alisons block, up in the lift, I'm guessing they'll be coming up right behind me. Down the corridor. I ring the doorbell. I ring the doorbell. Kick the door and ring the doorbell.

SHUGHIE Alison quick, give us that suitcase, I have to run, I've got business to do. Aye, all of a sudden I'm a business man. I'm no shouting at ye. I love you. I'll explain in Donegal. Down the corridor, lift doors open, two punters get out, they look at the suitcase. They want my money. Well they're not going to get it. Do you know who I am? The name's O'Donnell, Shughie O'Donnell, Shughie kill or be killed O'Donnell. I'm no afraid to use this so back off or you're dead meat. I press the lift button, the doors close, I nearly faint. Down at the bottom the doors open, I'm out of here like a greyhound out of a trap. Running up the street I look behind me, they're still after me. I jump on a wee bike outside a sweet shop. It was only when I'm sitting on it I realised how small it is. My knees are knocking off my chin. I look behind me, there's a ten year old chasing me, behind him the other two punters. A taxi pulls up, folks get out, I jump in. "Take me to Stranraer. I know it costs a lot of money, I've got a lot of money. What's with all the questions? It's got to do with the peace process and you are fucking it up!"

We arrive in Stranraer. "Aye I've got a tip for you, get elocution lessons."

I'm standing in the car park eating a bag of chips and I spot the BMW. Luckily they don't spot me. I get indigestion. I throw the bag of chips away. Half a bag left, I don't care. Climb into the back of a lorry before they see me, it's full of sheep. They're all looking at me. It's a crime how many sheep they squeeze into the one lorry. One, two, three, zzzzz

When I wake up the lorry's driving off the ferry at Larne. What if the RUC search this lorry and find me with a gun in my pocket and a suitcase full of money? It's to do with the peace process officer! I don't think so. *(Affirms)* I am invisible to the RUC, I am invisible to the RUC, I am invisible to the RUC, and it works. The lorry drives down the road for about ten miles and pulls into a wee garage. I get out, buy some antiperspirant. I'm starting to smell of sheep and everything. Phone a taxi, get into the taxi, tell the man where I'm going and fall asleep. When I wake up, before I even open my eyes, I know where I was. I could feel it in every atom of my being. I'm home. Safe and dry. It was a Zen taxi moment. Even the grass blades at the side of the road look sexy in Donegal. And I'm a rich man and this is what my Granda always wanted; to come back to Donegal a rich man. I'm a genetic success story.

SHUGHIE Up there to the left pal.

I'm going to spend the next fortnight in the poshest bed in the poshest room in the poshest hotel in Donegal with Alison. Drinking champagne, smoking Havana cigars and making plans 'cos the world is my oyster, and I like oysters.

Pull up here pal.

I know it is the middle of nowhere, I like the middle of nowhere.

When he drove off there wasn't another sinner in sight only me and a Bumble bee, couple of wee birds, loads of butterflies, sounds of the river, there's a rabbit. In fact it was quite busy, it was like a fucking metropolis. Mother Nature in all her splendour and I'm part of it. I walked up that hill and the minute I walked in I knew I belong here, I'm home. Obviously I'm gonny have to knock it down and build a house… but I can… cause I'm a rich man. I'm a rich man waiting for a beautiful woman. Waiting. Waiting. And I'm sick of waiting. *(Goes to door and looks down the hill)* You're going to miss the best bit Alison *(blocks the door with mine barrel and chair)*.

(Suitcase is on top of first barrel. He slowly flicks the safety catches and slowly lifts the lid. He is deadpan. Closes the lid and stares straight in front of him still deadpan. Opens the lid again. Pauses and then pulls out a plastic bag)

Willy the wino's plastic bag.

(He drops it on the ground and then proceeds to slowly remove a large book with "Yoga" written large on the cover, drops it on the ground and removes four other self-help books one by one, dropping them all on a pile on the floor. Turns and pulls away the barrel that blocks the door, he exits.)

Fuuuuuuuuuuuuuuuuuuuuuuuuuuuuck!!!

(Enters furious and distressed)

The bitch, she stole my money. Never trust a hippy. I've been burned by the woman I love. I don't believe it. Bitch. Wait a minute slow down Shughie she never, she fucking did, she stole my money. I don't believe this. *(Considering)* Wait a minute, she's a Presbyterian Buddhist, it's not her style. This is the woman you want to make babies with Shughie get a grip. Phone her mother. Don't. You'll only get into trouble. That's the pattern. Alison does something peculiar under the pretext it's sensible, I react and I'm the bad guy. *(Sits on wooden box)*

How dare you accuse me of stealing money. Shughie O Donnell I've a good mind to dump you. I was minding it because you can't be trusted with it. The last time you were on that boat you spent fifty pounds on a slot machine.

Well I don't need you to mind my money! She's probably got it changed into travellers' cheques by now.

When she arrives I won't even mention it. I'll let her bring it up. It's only money Alison, don't get so uptight.

(Picks up book from the floor)

"Relationships. Understanding your relationships through the four temperaments" *(drops it and picks up another)* "You can heal your life" *(opens it randomly)* "in the infinity of time where I am all is perfect" *(drops it, annoyed, and picks up another)* "Money is my friend" *(reading back cover)* "Does money slip through your fingers with ease?" *(Frustrated and full of contempt, he drops it and picks up another)* "Relaxation" – do you know what would relax me now hen? My fucking money! *(Drops it and picks up another)* "The Gentle Art of Yoga"? What's so gentle about sticking your legs behind your head? *(He sees a slip of paper protruding from the pages, and pulls out a short letter)* Ah, a wee note… *(before he reads it)* If you liked the Da Vinci Code you'll love Alison McKay.

(Begins to read silently, grows perplexed reads aloud, slowly)

"Dear Shughie, I hope you had a good journey." *(Looks up in disbelief)* "I suppose you're wondering what happened the money." *(Pauses, looking confused, slowly re-reads)* "Dear Shughie, I hope you had a good journey. I suppose you're wondering what happened the money." (Reads the next line silently but can't comprehend so re-reads it aloud, clinically) "There-were-bad-vibes-off-that-money…Shughie". *(Exasperated)* There were bad vibes off that money! Don't be stupid Alison. "By the time you read this note…" *(Goes back to the start of the note trying to understand the context, certain he must be misunderstanding something)*

"Dear Shughie, I hope you had a good journey. I suppose you're wondering what happened the money. There-were-bad-vibes-off-that-money-Shughie. By-the-time-you-read-this-note… I-will-have-given-it… *(re-reads)* I-will-have-given-it…to the Sudan famine appeal… It's for the higher good. Someday-you-will- thank-me-for this. Love Alison, kiss, kiss."

Kiss kiss?

(Reading fast, furious and incredulous)

"Dear Shughie, I hope you had a good journey. I suppose you're wondering what happened the money. There were bad vibes off that money Shughie. By the time you read this note… I will have given it to the Sudan famine appeal. It's for the higher good. Someday you will thank me for this." I don't believe it.

That was my fucking money. *(Jumps up and pulls out the mobile phone)* You've got a boundary problem hen. You better have kept a bloody receipt. See how good you are at writing letters when you have to write them a letter asking them for the money back.

(Pushes buttons)

C'mon. Hurry up, the battery's going. Hello Mrs McKay, it's Shughie here. Is Alison there Mrs Mc Kay? She's watching TV. Could you tell her to come to the phone? Could you tell her to come to the phone please Mrs. McKay. I'm here in Donegal. Mrs. McKay tell Alison to come to the phone. I'm not angry. The weather's fucking lovely. Tell Alison to come to the fucking phone! *(Phone dies)*

I don't believe it. Do I look like Bob Geldof. My money, I'm a poor man. I hope they Africans appreciate what I have been through. *(Sits on box stunned)*

(Stands up, takes out last cigarette from a crumpled box. Crushes box, drops it. Tries to light the cigarette with lighter which weakly sparks but never ignites. Tries in vain to fix it by shaking it, he flings the lighter on the floor, breaks the cigarette in two and drops it. Sits on box a broken man. Picks up Willie's plastic bag and empties it, on top of the debris is a box of matches, he picks up the broken cigarette and lights it.)

SHUGHIE Willie I'm going to get a mass said for you. I don't believe it. You're not dead ten minutes and already you're working miracles. *(Spots a naggin of Jamesons, opens it and offer a toast)* Yer health! *(Realising his insensitivity)* Sorry. To the afterlife! *(Takes a slug which packs a big kick)* Jesus, Willie what did you put in this? A bit of a blend. Never mind cheeky it's bloody aggressive. *(Discovers small silver ashtray)* What are you like? Bit of a dark horse you were. *(Uses ashtray, picks up a postcard)* Nice wee picture... Donegal. I can see it now. Friday night, *(holds up shirt and tie)* put on your clean shirt and yer tie, walk down Argyle street meet a young lady, invite her back to your cardboard box for an aperitif and to look at your art collection. *(Realising he's being disrespectful)* Sorry. I didn't mean to take the piss. I've had a hard couple of days. You had a hard couple of days yourself but at least you're past the worst of it. I'm in no position to take the piss out of you. *(Picking up sock)* I tell you it's a sad day when a dead man's got cleaner socks than the ones I am wearing. *(noticing the bulk inside it)* Here Willie, I hope you didn't leave your foot behind you.

(Pulls out a big fat wad of rolled notes)

Fifty pound notes!!!!

THE END

His Master's Voice

RURAL ELECTRIC

Introduction

Little John Nee

The parish hall
Growing dark in the sunset
With no electric

It was Angela McLaughlin of this parish what made Rural Electric happen, she commissioned the show for the Earagail Arts Festival. When we talked about possible themes for a show I immediately thought of the "electrifying". I had played with the notion of doing an outdoor spectacle based on the history of Donegal, I don't mind saying this was inspired by Royale de Luxe's "History of France". The images of men raising poles stuck with me, so when I talked to Angela I already had notions.

I had just finished a tour of Scotland with "Salt o' the Earth" and although it was in many ways a comic show it had its roots in the despair I witnessed on the streets of Glasgow in recent times. So I was up for some fun and illuminations. I wrote many haiku's about the parish and characters of the fictitious "Meenamore"

A new dynamo
On the old bicycle wheel
The bright beam of light

When it came time to write the show the characters all stepped forward and simply got on with it, some were shy at first, so let them alone, I didn't force them to reveal themselves. Fr. Murphy was one such character. There was always something funny about him alright but I never suspected his dark past.

Laura Sheeran agreed to do the music. No better woman. It was the first time that I had someone else singing in one of my shows. I was aware that I was taking a huge risk by having her sing, because I knew the rest of the show would then have to come up to that standard.

I had a lot of ideas about how I needed the set to work. I was fortunate that Mike Regan was available to make the magic happen, another artist that enriches my life unquantifiably! A show about the electrification would want to have good lightening, thank you Aidan Wallace.

The show premiered in St. Mary's Hall, Dungloe one fine summers evening. People travelled for miles. One of the great joys of the Earagail Festival is that its not confined to one town and you're are likely to spend the duration driving through some of the most beautiful countryside in the world on your way to see a show. Your head is already full of it before the show begins.

At times it can be difficult creating "Rural Theatre". If you're looking for wealth and fame you might be better looking elsewhere, but the rewards more than compensate and it's what I love doing. We performed Rural Electric in a hall in Clonmany in Inishowen. As is common the set up was hard work, it wasn't a well equipped theatre venue. There was sunlight flooding in from windows twenty foot off the ground around the hall; we needed complete darkness. Ladders, silage wrap and gaffer tape one hour till show time. It's always worth it, even if there's little glory in it. A week later there was a five star review for the show in the Guardian newspaper right beside a review of Swan Lake in Covent Garden. You do the work because you love it, you never know what will become of it.

RURAL ELECTRIC

The show begins in a rural parish hall in Donegal in the present day. The set comprises of an unremarkable plain grey wall with grooved 1950's timber. To the front, stage right, there is a corner piece of the same material. This creates an entrance space. On the stage left side of the grey wall there is an old fuse board. Just after the fire announcement there is a bang and flash from the fuse board and the hall is plunged into darkness.

Scene 1: Intro

>   (*Power cut*)

CARETAKER (*entering stage right and lighting a match*) Has anyone a match? Is the smokers all outside? Is the fella was doing the talk about the electric here? Do you know anything bout electric or do you just talk about it? (*Match goes out, exits stage right*)

LJ (*Enters stage right lights match*) Well Barney, I know nothing about nothing but I console myself with the wise words of Albert Einstein "imagination is more important than knowledge". Now where's the fuseboard? (*Finds an oil lamp beside fuse board and lights it*)

Fr. Murphy's lamp. He wasn't the worst of them. Though I've heard it said he was fond of dipping his wick.

>   (*Opens hinged door; covers the fuse board and presenting a shelved wall with religious paraphernalia and revealing an old gramophone, this is the parochial house. Gramophone plays 'Arlene'. L.J. exits*)

Scene 2: The Parochial House

(Fr. Murphy enters, in cassock, grey hair/dodgy wig and a black eye patch, begins to dance before catching himself and turning off the gramophone)

FATHER MURPHY There's no such thing as a harmless dance. Dance with yourself and you dance with the devil. Betrayed by my own two feet.

The day started out innocent enough. I went to Derry to the cinema, "Some like it hot", O Marilyn, Marilyn Monroe, dear God why did you create a woman like Marilyn if you didn't want us to lust after her?

On the way home I came by Creeslough – a common enough mistake – I saw a woman in an upstairs window, pulling the curtains, the electric light behind her. It wasn't so much the woman as it reminded me of another time in another place... another woman.

Curse those bright lights of Creeslough!

> *(Sings)* **The Bright Lights of Creeslough**
> **There are thoughts inside my head**
> **But I keep them to myself**
> **I don't want to go to hell**
>
> **The bright lights of Creeslough**
> **Could lead a man astray**
> **The bright lights of Creeslough**
> **Would lead a man astray**

Everybody all together now! That boy at the back! Stand up and sing!

> **The bright lights of Creeslough**
> **Could lead a man astray**
> **The bright lights of Creeslough**
> **Would lead a man astray**

(Father Murphy exits)

Scene 3: Dark Donegal

(*LJ enters*)

LJ Fr. Murphy is engulfed by his own dark thoughts, his own dark shame in the bleak black unforgiving night; in this parish accustomed to darkness, where every house has a host of dancing shadows on the kitchen walls and every family familiar with those shapes that loiter in the corner of bedrooms.

And for many the darkness is a comfort. The end of a hard day's toil. A womblike place safe in a safe universe, but for many more it is a doorway into the dark night of the soul, a gateway to purgatory and long lonely suffering, and Donegal had its fair share of darkness...

Scene 4: Epic ESB

But help is on the way... thanks to the brave boys and girls of the Electricity Supply Board. (*Puts on woolly hat*)

In the forests of Finland trees are felled and floated downstream to the fjords to be loaded on boats, the boats battle across the stormy North Sea for the ports of the emerald isle, Dublin, Limerick and Cork.

(*Pulls off tarpaulin to reveal cable reel*)

The poles are unloaded and creosoted – treated with creosote, and loaded onto lorries which wind their way along windy roads to the remotest parts of the island! Except for those remote places where the roads are too windy, like Donegal. So the poles were loaded onto smaller boats that battled up the stormy west coast to the piers of Donegal.

Excited crowds thronged to witness the delivery of the creosoted poles.

(*Hoists a rope front of stage pulling up the E.S.B. poles*)

All along the northlands, groups of local E.S.B. men assemble on the beaches to play their part in history. Donegal's finest and fittest, recently trained in the ways of electrification. They know no fear, though for many the greatest challenge is the prospect of getting out of bed in the morning, a strange new experience.

Bravely the work is begun, but sometimes unexpectedly it rains, many get wet. More have to cower under cover until the rain stops, with nothing to nourish them only tea and sandwiches... and biscuits. These are the men that liberated us from darkness – let us not forget them.

(Puts up pole stage right)

They were given no medals, their heroism unsung. In Hollywood they were still regurgitating the deeds of the marines in the South Pacific, in Donegal our own Iwo Jima went unnoticed.

(Puts up pole stage left, pausing half way to create iconic Iwo Jima image.)

But they were not all brutish men.

(Unrolling green muslin from the cable reel with the grace of a ballet. Three sections of muslin are drawn from this real and hung from the poles and set to create rolling hills as the following is described...)

Many were sensitive and creative, light of foot and soft of hand, they skipped over the green hills from parish to parish in advance of the work parties persuading the locals of the benefits of electric. They too were brave in the face of relentless cynicism. "Sure they've had electric in Buncrana since 1904 and they're still the same as they were without it".

Against all odds the E.S.B. swept through the land putting up poles.

(A string is pulled on the set that lifts a line of little poles across the top of the set.)

(Sings) **Meenamore**
There's a little Irish parish
Up in the Irish hills
With honest Irish people
Irish boys and Irish girls
There's a place 'tis known as Meenamore
Could not mean more to me
It's that little Irish parish without the ESB

Scene 5: A Sweeping View of the Parish

(Using hats, props and small costume changes we meet the following characters in situ...)

Paddy Dubh opens a parcel from America, to find a fifty dollar tweed jacket, puts it on and finds fifty dollars in the pocket "**where would we be without the yanks?**", He draws on a cigarette with his long brown twisted fingers; and fills his long brown twisted lungs with smoke, then reluctantly lets it go. **"It's my smoke I paid for it. Where would we be without the yanks?"**

His son Pat Dubh, Paddy's Boy, **"with a bag of kittens going down to the river to drown the little buggers."**

Bridie Diver **"born nearly a hundred years ago – well eighty anyway- born into a cartload of fish in Killybegs, my mother said I couldn't wait, my father was the seventh son of a seventh son and so I have the gift, I have visions. Every morning I empty the tea leaves into the yard and read the news before the hens eats them."**

Joe Duffy wraps a parcel of ham at the back of the grocery van then cuts a fresh plug of tobacco. Thinking about women.

Mc Groarty's 2 year old heifer chewing cud watching a crow out of the side of her eye. The crow on a post looks back at her. The cow looks at the crow and the crow looks at the cow. Day after day, week after week, month after month, the cow looks at the crow and the crow looks at the cow. Who knows what they're thinking? We'll never know! Shoo!

Jim Mc Groarty goes over the hill. In five minutes he'll find a dead lamb.

Meanwhile Dubhs' Dog skulks into the yard after being out all night, blood on her coat, a guilty look on her face. *(whistling)*

Joe Duffy struggles to get the grocery van up the hill in third gear, thinking not about the woman he's engaged to Kitty Mc Gonagle but thinking instead about Susie Diver...

Ah God sure we're all thinking about Susie Diver...

Scene 6: Susie Diver

LJ Susie Diver, how to describe her? Susie Diver lives with her grandmother Bridie. But more than that Susie Diver lives in the mind of every man in a twenty mile radius of Meenamore. She lives in the heart of every man ever saw her. Susie Diver sure how could you describe her. I'll try.

(Dressing in skirt, shawl and wig produced from a tin bathtub)

Susie Diver dressed in clothes she had fashioned for herself, she had the fine hips of a Donegal woman which we all know are the finest in the world.

She had beautiful chestnut brown hair cut in a style that suited her.

She wore a shawl around her shoulders that made her look like the Colleen Bawn.

And every morning she'd gambol across the fields to fetch water from the well.

Little birds would fly beside her, circling around her head singing "Susie Diver, Susie Diver!"

And butterflies would fly close by her head, and if you had an expensive microphone you could hear their booming wings a hundred miles away "Susie Diver, Susie Diver!"

Salmon would leap from the river to catch a glimpse of Susie Diver.

The train would go by on its way to Burtonport "Susie Diver! Susie Diver! Susie Diver! Susie Diver!"

When she got to the well there was always at least two frogs waiting for her, **"Ah Susie give us a kiss! Go on I'm a prince give us a kiss and you'll see for yourself!"**

"Never you mind him, Susie, you'd know to look at him he's only an ould frog. I'm a real prince, Susie, trapped in a frog's body. Give us a kiss and we'll live happily ever after."

Fortunate for Susie she lived in a time when Irish women were unencumbered by the burdens of modern consumerism...

(Fetches tin bath tub - stage left hidden by the tarpaulin
Scrubs shirt with washboard
Fetches mangle and rings shirt
Returns tub, mangle and washboard to stage left all done laboriously to
appropriate musical accompaniment building frenetically.)

(Irons shirt. Poses: a picture of a happy domestic country woman.)

SOUND OF COWS TURNED ON

(Very stressed and barely in character, begins to run around removing the
green muslin and returning props, setting up the next scene. Opens the
fuse-box door to reveal a small red cottage door on the top half of the set.
Opens a grey panel door in the bottom half of the set to EXIT SUSIE DIVER.
L.J. reappears, wearing a bowler hat and playing a little harp (very Darby
O'Gill) leaning over the top half of the red cottage half door on the top half
of the set!)

SOUND OF COWS TURNED OFF

(Sings) **There's laughter and contentment in every Irish home,**
There's homemade jam and butter,
 On homemade soda scones,
There's happy reminiscences of golden days of yore,
In that little Irish parish... Meen-aah-more!

(Closes door)

Scene 7: Johnny Doherty visits

(LJ enter from the grey panel door in the bottom half of the set.)

LJ All the talk about electricity didn't impress me - I was hard to impress - I'd
seen plenty electric in Scotland. My Uncle Micky in Rathmullan had the
electric and he said it was no good; it was too bright. He wouldn't bother
turning the light on in the kitchen for that reason. What he used to do is
he'd have his chair in the kitchen outside the bedroom door, then he'd turn
on the light in the bedroom and sit in the kitchen reading his paper with
the light from the bedroom bleeding through.

There were lots of stories about old people who would only turn on the electric light to give them enough light to light their paraffin lamps, and when they had their lamp lit they'd turn off the electric.

There were plenty more didn't want the electric at all for they thought it would burn down the house.

I preferred the dim light of candles and lamps and turf fires. There were plenty unlit corners where a boy could sit unnoticed. I liked the way peoples faces changed according to what way the light hit them and how the shadows fell.

There was a man called to our house called Johnny Doherty, a travelling man with his parcel of tools under his arm he'd make things out of tin and mend what needed mending. After he'd had a bite to eat he'd take out his fiddle and spend the evening playing tunes and telling yarns and if we were very lucky he'd play and dance at the same time.

I loved the way the reflection of the turf fire would flash in his eyes when he'd be telling stories, and behind that the bright light that must have been there since the day he was born, the brightest light I ever seen…so like I say after that I was hard to impress. But then one day the lorries came…

Scene 8: The epic comes to the village

There were two big lorries, well one big lorry and a tractor with a trailer full of poles.

Big E.S.B. men with gnarled hands and gnarled faces jumped off the lorry with sledgehammers, shovels and picks and all sorts of electrical accoutrements.

Word went out and a crowd gathered. Barking children and old people wagging their tails, pushing and poking to get a good view…
"What in under God are they going to do?"

That was the first time I laid eyes on George McLoughlin. I'd never seen nothing like him before, he was like a film star; last one to jump off the lorry, slow and smooth…

(Puts on donkey jacket, neckerchief and Woody Guthrie hat)

He swung around and looked at me and said
"Do you want a bubble gum?"

I was so enamoured with him I followed him around all day watching him work.

(Moody does his moves, rock'n'roll putting up a pole (short pole used for top of pole scene)

At the end of the day I followed him home. All the other men were staying in lodgings but George McLoughlin had a caravan all of his own.

(Pulls out the caravan steps at stage right entrance exits...enters coming down the steps with a guitar.)

(Moody sings) **Mr. Electricity**
My name is George McLoughlin I come from Inishowen
I don't need nobody I'm happy on my own
I'm like a shooting star, I'm a real live wire
You can call me Mr. Electricity

I got power in my fingertips, got electric in my blood
Gonna shock your daddy baby
Gonna light your neighbourhood
You can call me Mr. Electricity

My name is George McLoughlin I come from Inishowen
I don't need nobody I'm happy on my own
I'm like a shooting star, I'm a real live wire
You can call me Mr. Electricity

MOODY Don't really call me Mr. Electricity, my name's George McLoughlin but my friends call me Moody, you can call me Moody.

Don't call me Mr. Electricity people would only laugh.

Scene 9: Moody and Susie meet

ʟᴊ George McLoughlin up a pole watching the world below.

ᴍᴏᴏᴅʏ *(to audience)* I see things different from other people. I have my own unique perspective. I have the eagle eye view. People say I'm odd. I don't care.

One thing annoys me is when people say "O Elvis!"

Fuck you and fuck Elvis. I'm a Gene Vincent man. Thons the boy. For I'm different, born different, I don't run wi the pack, I'm a lone wolf. A lone wolf wi an eagle eye.

I see things different. Sometimes I look out at them cables stretching out reaching out, and it seems to me they're like arms and hands reaching out joining up, that's how the power flows and I think if only people could do that more often…

We'll try that now. I want you to all put your hands in the air like electricity poles. Now hold hands with the person on either side of you! That's it create an electrical circuit. Feel the power. Look at that poor man there not able to put up his hands, we'll have a whip round after and send him to Lourdes. That's it feel the power feel the electricity coursing through your veins…

Wouldn't catch me doing that for I'm a lone wolf. No notion of holding hands till I saw her.

> *(Towards Susie down below on the road)*

Hello how are ye doing down there. Just you stay stood where you're stood and I'll be right down to you, don't go away now.

> *(Slides down the pole)*

How are you. My name's George McLoughlin but people call me Moody I work up the poles, I have a different point of view from most folks…I'm not like other men. Elvis? Oh aye. Aye I love Elvis aye. Did you ever hear tell of Gene Vincent? No?

Elvis is good alright. You live up in that wee house I saw ye. Stand in, there's that flookin' eejit in the grocery van it's a miracle he doesn't run over somebody. Stand in. The eejit, he's after splashing your legs. You stand still I'll soon sort that out.

> *Moody goes down on one knee to wipe the mud from her leg with his neckerchief... gets lost in the act... before snapping back to reality, stands up*

Oh sorry about that! Here look you wipe your own legs, you're better used to it than me and I'll just go up this pole where I belong!

Scene 10: Pickled Trouts' Eyes

> *(Puts on Bridie's red scarf and house coat...)*

"Bridie Diver born nearly a hundred years ago..."

> *(Whips back the headscarf...)*

500 yards up the road the O'Malley sisters, and Patricia McCann and Mary McCallion arrive at Bridie Diver's cottage looking for tea, but sure them girls had no interest in tea, they were after news. They gulped back the tea and showed the cups to Bridie, **"tell us about the electric, Bridie!"**

Bridie looked at the leaves. **"Cows will milk themselves... and kettles will boil themselves."**

"God Bridie what do we care about cows and kettles? Tell us something we want to hear, tell us about the men!"

Bridie got thick at that, went to the shelf and brought down a jar of pickled trouts' eyes, undid the lid poured them onto a plate and gave them a swirl. Bridie looked at the trouts' eyes and the trouts' eyes looked right back at her

Bridie sees the world she knows
The parish hall with no electric
Growing dark in the sunset
The last of the light creeping in

And the smell of parafin
Bridie sees houses with the thatch fell in
Where once lived men and women
Who owned nothing only children
Too many of them
And nothing to feed them
This place scarred with the grief
Of young people leaving
Endless people leaving going foreign to make a living
To become strangers in strange lands
How will they be met and how will they be treated?

Bittersweet this place that holds in its embrace so much pain
The damned and their secrets
The hurt and the shame
And Bridie sees the change
Big posters showing
Silver toasters shooting toast
In shiney Formica kitchens...
Delighted women in brand new drip dry bry-nylon
Smiling!
All the style

Bridie sees the Acceleration
Bridie sees a nation full of electric contraptions
Things she has no name for
Things she wouldn't know what to do with them if she had them
Vacuum cleaners and dishwashers
Cappuccino makers
There's foreigners coming
Leaving behind their own hard times and their own loved ones
To become strangers in strange lands
How will they be met?
How will they be treated?
Bridie sees the big screen
The proliferation of the television
Lying politicians
Soaps and propaganda
Salvation and salivating
Bridie sees African starvation

Bridie sees hungry hungry Irish men channel hopping
Looking for porn
Bridie sees the hidden desperation and the visible desolation
Boys racing, rubber burning, overturning.
Young men hanging dead of loneliness
Young girls puking
Falling comatose, too pissed
To stop their skirts being lifted
Bridie sees it all
And the girls say "What do you see Bridie, tell us what you see!"

BRIDIE *(big pause)* You're going to get married. You'll have two children a boy and a girl. And you're going to be very happy.

Scene 11: Just another day in Meenamore

LJ Meanwhile 500 yards down the road Moody McLoughlin
Stuck up the pole.
Eagle eyes spies Kitty McGonagle
Who coincidentally is – speaking figuratively – also...
So to say... just returning from a visit to the doctor in Letterkenny with shocking news.
Kitty takes a wee turn, jumps of the road and goes behind a whin bush to vomit.
Moody McLoughlin – compassionate man – slides down the pole
And appears by her side to console, **Are ye aright pet?**
At that precise moment who arrives only
The O'Malley sisters, and Patricia McCann and Mary McCallion
They look at Moody and Kitty,
They look at Moody, they look at Kitty
They look at each other and draw a conclusion.
Just as they are drawing their conclusion
Who draws up in his grocery van
Spotting only a bunch of girls at the side of the road and deciding the moment opportune
Failing to see his fiancée...
Joe Duffy.
How yees girls what's the craic?

Kitty steps forward and says Joe I'm pregnant
Joe takes a few steps swings back and lets go
Hits Moody on the nose. *(Singing birds)*
Moody crumples on the floor. The girls scream!
I didn't hit him that hard says Joe.
The girls point behind him.
Fucking fuck I forgot to put the fucking brake on the fucking van and now the fucking van is rolling down the fucking hill. Joe ran to catch the van.
Shortly thereafter Susie arrives **What happened here girls?**
The girls explain about Joe and his van
And how Moody was hit
And how they had found **Moody and Kitty**
Behind a bush... Naked!
Doing it!
And now Kitty is having a baby!
Well says Susie. **Car chases, mindless violence and meaningless sex!**
Just another day in Meenamore!

Scene 12: Moody at confession

(Places little grill low on wall, goes on knees)

MOODY Bless me Father for I have sinned, it's a good while since I was at confession Father, I don't do that much out of the way Father and to tell you the truth Father I'm here now not so much for what I've done as for what people have said I've done but I never done Father if ye get my drift. There's people saying I got a local girl pregnant if you'll excuse the language father but like I say I never laid a hand on her. Don't get me wrong I'm fond of women Father I'd be a poor candidate for the priesthood, oh I'd have the occasional sinful thought alright father in fact I'm demented with desire for a local woman right enough but I like to think it's a healthy thing father.

What's her name? Eh... Susie Diver.

Slow down Father it's only ambitious thoughts I've been having there's been no sinning Father... Our Father who art in heaven.

Scene 13: The truth about Fr. Murphy

FR. MURPHY I first went to the United States in 1928 with a gang of lads from home. We got work straight away laying cable in South Boston. I became an "electric man" work hard, play hard, no end of fun, thought it couldn't get any better then I met her. I'll never forget her. Mary Diver. In my heart forever...

I'll never forget the feel of her skin below my fingers, I'll never forget the one and only night we spent together in that cheap hotel on the eastside of Boston. I see her fresh as a picture framed in the window as she pulled the curtains and reached to switch off the light.

She said **"I wonder where the electric goes."** Then climbed into bed and said "now I know". We loved till the daylight. I loved her till I had no love left to give her. I loved her and I left her...

I left her to go laying cable, knee deep in the mud of south Boston, we worked a late shift in the rain. After work I went straight to the bar with the boys from home for some beer. The beer led to whiskey and the whiskey led to cards. I was sitting beside a pal of mine Martin McGlynn, I went to school with him.

He says to me **"Murphy I notice you didn't come back to the lodgings last night. My guess is you spent the night with that doll of yours. Well I don't blame you! She has the finest pegs in all of Boston!"**

(Change to parochial house)

Mind your tongue Martin, mind your tongue. We played more cards and drank more whiskey. He was winning and I was losing. Sometime in the small hours we staggered out into the street. We ducked down a lane for a leak. Martin says to me

"I can't get the picture of that doll of yours out of my head, the finest pegs in Boston!"

I flung him up agin the wall "mind your tongue Martin!"

It was then that Shorty came up behind me, smashed a bottle on the back of my head. Did me no harm. But I done him harm. I whipped out my blade and plugged it between his ribs. I twisted and pulled it out. I swung round and stuck it deep into Martin's heart.

I dropped it and started walking. Walking. I kept walking. I had to get out of Boston. I knew I was walking away from the only reason life was worth living, I kept walking.

A couple of days later on the journey south I was in another bar drunk again. Caught sight of a pretty girl out of the corner of my eye, gave her a smile and a wink of that eye.

Immediately I was overwhelmed with remorse, like I'd betrayed the only woman I'd ever loved. I remembered the priest back home, he used to say "if thy eye offendeth thee, pluck it out…"

I was ordained in Mexico City in 1935. But I couldn't get her out of my mind. Mary Diver. I went back to Boston to see if I could find her. Mary Diver? Mary Diver died in child labour, had a daughter, Susan, they brought her back to the old country to her Grandmother, Bridie…in a place called Meenamore.

Dear God I swore I would never kill again but how can I let her throw her life away on a damned electric man!

(Exits)

SOUND OF THUNDER, FLASH OF LIGHTNING

Scene 14: Susie sings by the window

(Enter Susie wrapped in her shawl, she opens the fuse-board and the red door to reveal a window. She hangs Moody's hanky on a small washing line across the window.)

MUSICIAN/FEMALE VOICE SINGS

Look see the broken sky
Draining down into the streams
My man in a caravan
I hold you in my dreams
Wish that I had more
I wish that I had more
Look see the broken sky...

SOUND OF THUNDER, FLASH OF LIGHTNING

Scene 15: Joe Duffy's foul work

LJ   Joe Duffy drives his van through the pouring rain calling in on neighbours and relations stirring dark emotions with the help of cheap whiskey. He sits with the twelve Gallagher brothers, **"Time we done something about them E.S.B. boys swanning round here like they owned the place. That Moody McLoughlin, sniffing round our women, time he was taught lesson. What he needs is a good kicking and I'm the boy would give it to him."**

Joe Duffy calls to the Dubhs, the Donnells and his cousins' cousins fermenting hatred and bitterness, and the plan is laid down. **"Tomorrow night there's the dance in the parish hall, the official switching on of the electric, Moody Mc Loughlin will get what's coming to him. He'll be sorry he ever laid eyes on Meenamore."**

Joe Duffy drives his grocery van through the sheets of rain, he passes a caravan with a candle in the window...

SOUND OF THUNDER, FLASH OF LIGHTNING

Scene 16: Moody in his caravan

(Sings) **She's an unnatural high**
She's the reason why
I'm satisfied
Oh I can't wordify.

Baby I can't help myself
I can't help myself
I can't help myself.
The fix it book is on the shelf
But I can't fix myself
I can't fix myself…

She's an unnatural high
She's the reason why I'm satisfied.

SOUND OF THUNDER, FLASH OF LIGHTNING

Scene 17: The dance, the electric, the showdown

*(*LIGHTS DROPPED*. Hatch opens on front corner-piece to create box-office.)*

That was the last night the parish hall smelled of paraffin. Crowds came from all over the hall was filled and the band started playing…

Country Singer:
There's half a chicken sandwich in the pocket of my coat
The arse out of my trousers was eaten by a goat
There's fleas in my mattress there's holes in my shoes
But when it comes to loving I'm the man for you

Thank you thank you, and now ladies and gentlemen boys girls I'm going to ask Fr. Murphy to come to the stage for the official turning on of the lights. Come on up Father. A big round of applause for Fr. Murphy! Ah come on yous can do better than that!

LJ Fr. Murphy climbed onto the stage, looking tired and drawn like he'd been awake all night wrestling with his conscience. A black bag under his eye.

FATHER MURPHY I'd like to thank you all for coming tonight. Our lives are about to change now more than we can possibly tell. There shall be new temptations placed on our path that we are unprepared for, new opportunities for committing age old sins. I wish you all prosperity and happiness in the bright days ahead.

LJ The band started playing and the crowds flocked onto the floor. There was waltzing and fox-trotting, swinging and swirling. Moody and Suzie took to the floor together, facing each other. Looking, smiling, moving, touching, smelling, dancing, feeling, loving, together, oblivious to the men gathered around the edges of the hall, glowering. Evil eyes focused on the outsider.

(The men around the edges of the dance floor throw shapes)

LJ In a corner of the hall the evilest eye of them all, Fr. Murphy. If looks could kill Susie would be dancing with a dead man.

(NATIONAL ANTHEM PLAYS. A drunk struggles to stand to attention.)

Susie turned to Moody. **"I'll just go and get my coat, you wait outside for me."**

I was already outside staring at the moon, I turned to Moody
"Do you think there's anyone up there?"
"I'm fucking sure of it!"

We were that busy looking at the moon that we didn't notice the gang of men gathered around us, the smell of bloodlust in the air. I'd seen the look in their eyes only once before, at an abattoir. There was going to be a killing tonight.

Moody took a step forward, clenched his fists, threw out his chest, he looked straight into their eyes, like he was saying you might get me but I'll kill the first three men that come near me.

Joe Duffy knew no fear, he moved forward for his pound of flesh, but Fr. Murphy pushed past him like he wanted to be the first. He moved slowly through the circle right up to Moody face to face, their breaths mingled, he looked him in the eye, stuck out his hand, **"put it there I used to be an electric man myself"** he swung around, took a stand beside Moody.

Next thing in walked Susie. We formed a line, but nothing would stop Joe. He stepped forward, swaggered right up to Moody, swung back and let go, bang on the nose. Moody folded on the floor. I looked up there was a bottle flying through the air! What kind of a person would throw a bottle at a priest? Whoever it was was a bad shot, for the bottle hit me.

BLACKOUT

Rock a bye baby on the tree top
When the wind blows
The cradle will rock

Scene 18: After the fight

LIGHTS UP

LJ When I woke up I was being cradled in Susie's arms. I was only six years old but already I knew there's times to be cradled in a woman's arms and there's times you have to stand on your own two feet like a man. I jumped up. Moody was still lying on the ground rubbing his bloody nose. I looked around at a scene of devastation, blood and torn shirts, broken faces and broken heads; Susie and Fr. Murphy had annihilated the opposition. It was a massacre, moaning bodies all over the place. Fr. Murphy nursed his bruised knuckles, **"Stand up and fight!"**

Susie threw down the lump of wood she had used so well and helped Moody to his feet. He was weak around the knees, but he leaned against Susie and she led him off down the road away from the bright lights of the parish hall and past McGroarty's snoring cow.

I stayed stood looking at the moon. Someday mankind would land up there and when they did they'd need the Donegal men to do the tunnelling, Moody McLoughlin could put in the electric, and sure, they'd have to bring Johnny Doherty up to entertain us. And at the end of the night the three of us would stand outside and point down to the bright lights of Meenamore.

Meanwhile down the road Moody was feeling a bit woosie, Susie helped him to sit down on the ditch. Then she took the initiative flung her arms around him and planted a kiss on his lips. That's when the electric really kicked in, eyes lit up, sparks flying, all kinds of feelings been generated, that's when it happened, in a few short seconds Moody and Susie were lying in the ditch doing the rural electric.

I was still looking at the stars pondering the magnificence of it all, concluding that rural electric is all there is, even the great cities of the world, were built on rural electric, and I know if Albert Einstein was here tonight in this hall he'd probably turn around to me and say **"you're dead right the universe in it's very essence is rural and we are all of us ultimately motivated by that primal force "Rural Electric"**

I'd say well whatever you say Albert you're the smart one!

Scene 19: Epilogue (Bridie)

(Bridie turns the front corner piece around to reveal an interior corner of a country cottage from the fifties with sacred heart hanging on the wall and stark bare light bulb hanging from the ceiling.

Bridie looking intently at the bulb turns the light on. Then, staying stock still, and looking intently at the bulb, she turns it off. She is absorbed by the magic of it all, she turns the light off. She turns the light on. Turns the light off...)

THE END

THE MENTAL

Introduction

Little John Nee

At the end of my show "The Ballad of Jah Kettle" I left the hero Joe Boyle at the tail end of a poteen binge, demented and hallucinating, just returned from New York with his best friend's ashes in a jam jar, insane on a disused railway line in Donegal. He builds a monument out of scrap.

Five years later when Brendan Hone approached me about doing a show about St.Conals I remembered a scene in "Jah Kettle" where Joe Boyle a drunk teenage punk passing the asylum in the wee small hours with his pal Danny Devine shouts "you'll never get us!"

Initially Brendan had hoped I could do a show based on the recollections of Fergus Cleary, a local legend, who had just retired from his job as a social therapist/psychiatric nurse in St Conals. The show was to be a joint commission between axis ballymun and the HSE and when I met Ray Yeates the Centre Director at axis I was convinced that this was a risk worth taking. The adventure began. After talking to Fergus Cleary it became apparent to me that he was an adept performer with a vibrant style of his own and no shortage of material. He needed to perform his story himself.

And I thought again about Joe Boyle and what might have happened to him after I had left him demented by the old railway. Turns out he went back to New York...

Because music was such an integral part of the story it was great when Ray informed me we could afford two musicians. Laura Sheeran created some of the music while I was still writing the show: she is one of my all time favourite musicians in the whole wide world and consistently inspires me. Nuala Ni Chanainn is another musician and singer I hold in the highest regard, I was familiar with her work since we played together in Circus Story with Macnas a long long time ago and her sean nos singing cuts straight to the soul. I had high expectations of them both but great artists always surpass our expectations. The Mental is worth seeing for the music alone.

Producers Roisin Mc Garr and Ray Yeates provided us with the resources that helped us create what I believe is a beautiful show, a set built by Mike Regan and a lightening design by Sinead Wallace and a production crew to die for.

The Mental also introduced me to axis ballymun, a most nourishing experience.

THE MENTAL

Set in the very recent past

Joe Boyle from Donegal was once a punk, he went to the United States in the Eighties where he sang in bands. Joe was first institutionalised in New York City, eventually he was brought home to Donegal by a family member.

He is now resident in St. Conals.

Scene 1

> (*Lights up on a bare, modestly decorated hospital common room, part of the old asylum, there is a window downstage left. A chair and a table centre upstage, a bed stage left, and a chair slightly left of centre stage.*)
>
> *LOW SINGLE NOTE PIANO MUSIC*
>
> (*Joe moves slowly half dancing in a world of his own as if with the music, creating a magical ambience that allows us to glimpse his grace.*)

JOE   Hank Williams, born 1923 Georgiana, Alabama; died in the backseat of a Cadillac 1953. Patsy Cline born 1923 Shenandoah Valley, West Virginia…

(*Noticing audience*)

Nobody can see you.

That's their bad luck.

I can.

Maybe that's mine.

> (*Sings*) **She was the belle of old Tir Conaill**
> **Her happy smile lit up my world**
> **My father said she never loved me**
> **For if she did why did she go?**
> **And all because the lady loves**

Some fancy box of chocolates
And all because the lady loves
Some fancy box of chocolates

(To audience)

I know well where I am. Under no illusion.

People are surprised at the breadth of my knowledge of a wide variety of subjects... They're too polite to say anything, but I can see them wondering "what it is that has a decent intelligent man like me in the mental?"

I be surprised too. How do they do so well in positions of power up and down the country and them so fucking stupid.

It was a long road that got me here.

Scene 2

(Joe standing beside exterior wall, turns to his audience)

JOE When I was a young fella it wasn't often that we'd be passing up this way...

But when we were we were well aware of where we were...

"What's them high walls for daddy?"

"That's to keep your mammy's family off the street."

The mystery of it all filled my imagination.

HAMMER HOUSE OF HORROR ORCHESTRA STRINGS

All kinds of mad boys beyond them walls.
Chained up so as they don't escape under the full moon
To kill innocent people.
Holy God if they all escaped at the one time.
That'd be some handling.
They'd have to get the army in from Rockhill.

When we'd be passing I'd be checking
To see there were no new holes in the walls.
They should put up barbed wire.

What if they burst out of their chains?
And came to kill us all in our sleep.
What class of man was my mother's brother Patrick?
He'd been in there nearly all his life.
At that time I had no notion I was heading in this direction myself.

Scene 3

JOE I remember been brought here as a wain for the agricultural
show in the asylum field.

The day began with my stepmother, scrubbing my neck.
Me standing in the sink in my pelt.
Me shiny clean in the kitchen, into my clean vest
And into my Sunday best.
With a dollop of Brylcreem rubbed onto my skull
A clean hanky and two shillings in the pocket of my jacket.
And into the backseat of the Anglia
Waiting for my father.
Danny Devine came down the road
My father asked him where he was going and told him to jump in.

By the time we got there.
The grass had already begun to turn to mud.
Cows and horses done that.
And tractors.
Tractors and trailers, horseboxes.
Tearing it up. Turning it up.
But thon is some field.
Sloping down towards the town.
Thon was some day.

There was stalls wi footballs, stalls wi horse harnesses,
stalls wi tin buckets, wee cages wi guinea fowl, wooden pens
wi bantam hens, odd breeds of sheep, a donkey mare in foal,
a big table full of plastic toys… and sweets

Raffle tickets
And the smell of chips and the smell of cows
Rosettes and silver cups
An ice-cream van.
I stood in cow dung in my brand new summer sandals…
Sweets sticking to my teeth and fingers.
This field of fields filled with a power of things
The likes of which I've never seen
And more that I had;
Big women wi big hats dressed up as if for mass,
Old farmers washed for the first time in months.
A constant coming and going
Sloping down towards the town.
So many pairs of good shoes
In a field that wanted nothing more or nothing less than Wellington boots.

All this in the asylum field, all behind the Mental walls.
The biggest building in town
With faces up at the windows looking down at us.
Us watching posh ponies jumping over wee fences.
I keep looking up to see if i can see my Uncle Patrick.
My new summer sandals covered in cow dung… now I'm in trouble.

Scene 4

(A featureless corridor, Joe contents himself pacing, looking at the floor. He looks up and notices audience as if he has been waiting…)

JOE 'Mon you wi me.
There's plenty to see.
Plenty room to walk here.

(Joe leads his tour along the corridor)

The lemon paint peeling
In the old part of the building where few pass to notice.
Gone are the days of pandemonium
And the smell of lime wash.
Gone the choirs of endless crying
Big keepers with big keys.

One of the men who came to decorate said:
"I'd say if them auld walls could talk they'd have some tales to tell"
But he didn't stop to listen...
And me all the time wishing,
Wishing them talking walls would shut the fuck up.

    (At the foot of the stairs)

There was seldom a time that I felt I ever belonged
I toyed with a notion that I belonged to another species,
From another planet far beyond the stars
Someday my people will come back and rescue me.
For my presence here is surely a mistake.
But they never did.
I'm on my own.

    (Moving up the corridor)

These walls talk...
No more than the tress outside they've seen it all
Time swimming by.
Proud bloody walls
Well built. Stone by stone upon stone on stone
By hungry men good at their work
Oh these walls talk, they never shut up.

This place here was built the same year as Castlebar
Eighteen sixty something.
An asylum for "Lunatics, vagrants and idiots" that was the purpose of this.
Before that everybody went to the workhouse or worse.
That's how it came to pass

What souls walked these floors, and hugged these walls,
What dreams were lost?
Walls that heard cries in the night...

Walls that heard things that will never ever be told
Walls that hold every fear ever known in stone
High walls, long halls,
Wild big echo hey.
Hey.

Down all the years
Through time and space
All that remains
The presence of living things
All held within these walls
Like the shroud of Turin.
All held detained therein.

Scene 5

(Beside downstage chair)

JOE Joe Green used to sit here day in day out.
Saying nothing to nobody.

Well Seosamh
Cad é mar atá tú?

First time I met Seosamh. I was with my father and Sally my stepmother.
We were up to tell my Uncle Patrick that my mother died in England. Sally
saw Seosamh and went over to talk to him, for he was one of her people
from down her part of the country. I hardly noticed him, for even then he
was nearly invisible. Sally told us all about him on the road home in the
car. "He used to be a school teacher but took to writing stupid auld books,
drove him mad".

Seosamh Mac Grianna from Ranafast, came here in 1959. He'd exhausted all
other possibilities. A lot like myself.

I remember reading him at school... I remember not reading him; I had
bigger fish to be frying.

I had no interest in the Irish language. I forgot the wee bit I learnt within a week of leaving school. The only time I used it subsequently was with Danny Devine in New York bars in clandestine conversations pertaining primarily to the purchase of illicit substances.

If you do a lot of walking sooner or later you start following in someone else's footsteps. There's parts of the floor here wore away with the medication shuffle. I was following in Seosamh footsteps a long while before I met him.

"Is óg i mo shaol a chonaic mé uaim é, an ród sin a bhí le mo mhian"

"Young in my life I saw before me that road which satisfied my desire"

He died before I arrived here. I walked in his footsteps long enough it was inevitable that we would meet and so we did.

For time and space are no obstacles to the creatively inclined. Time and space are only ditches on the road home, boundaries to lean upon. Our kindred spirits are drawn together by magnetic forces to partake in a joint destiny.

> *(Sits on chair, stooped)*

Seosamh sat here day in day out (smokes an invisible woodbine) saying nothing to nobody.

"Ní thiocfadh caint a bhaint asim. Ní labhair mé riamh ar an rud a bhí i m'intinn. Bhí mé a' cosaint m'anam."

"Nothing would make me talk. I never spoke about that thing which was on my mind. I was defending my soul"

I'm learning the Irish now. I have to; if I want to know what he wrote, the way what he wrote it I have to learn the Irish. I have everybody in here tormented asking them questions, tell me the Irish so I can hear the way it sounds, tell me the English of it so I can understand it. There's a nurse in here, Mary… from Dungloe. Mary from Dungloe! She's no picture. I had her tortured with questions – ye'll have to learn the Irish she says… for Seosamh wrote a lot before he shut up.

Loose on the streets a Dublin, wi a headful of literacy and books, picking cigarette butts off the pavement on the road from Dublin to Dun Laoghaire, making a sport out of it. Fillin' all your pockets. Out on a wee rowing boat in the moonlight crossing the Irish Sea. Weaving the woes of his wanderings in Wales into wondrous stories that would drag ye half a mile down the road to hear the finish of it. I need to know the Irish of it, the truth of it the way he wrote it, the poetry and the music. The music of the words of Seosamh Mac Grianna.

To you it might look like there's no one sitting there.
That would be right I suppose, but it'd be more wrong.

For if the mind is gifted with the ability to travel far and wide,
why give it boots of lead.

If all that separates us is time and space, what's to say that him that once sat there so long is not now still sat there in a more subtle form, more comfortable than ever he was.

Life's too short and too precious for me to be putting crude limitations on my perceptions.

The Ranafast Jack Kerouac. In all the history of Ireland was there ever such a grumpy bastard as you Seosamh.

Scene 6

(Early afternoon in the day room, a social hub)

LOUD RADIO. MID-ATLANTIC RADIO PRESENTER WAFFLING INANELY AND ANNOYINGLY ACCOMPANIED BY EXCRUCIATING JINGLES.

Sound waves come into the tympanic membrane where they're amplified...

Through transduction the sound waves become neural electro-chemical energy travelling to the auditory cortex,

Sound waves entering into our entire being.
Stimulating responses.

Could you turn down the radio a wee bit please Mary?

Please Mary could you turn down the radio?

They're not listening to it. Nobody's listening to it.
It's hurting my head.
Could you turn it off please?
Well go and fuck yourself then you cruel fucking bitch
Get away from me
Don't touch me, don't touch

(Blackout)

Scene 7

(Daytime in the sitting room. DULL DRONE MUSIC MODULATING PITCH. Joe, heavily medicated, sitting on a chair drooling. Lights change to signify the passing of time. Joe remains impassive throughout)

Scene 8

(Joe turns to audience...)

JOE Come on we'll go for a walk. Me and Seosamh always walk down this way for a bit of peace. Can you see him yet? Can you not see him? You never heard tell of him. There's not much talk about him now. Bad enough being forgot when you're dead, it's not nice being forgot about when you're still living, though Seosamh didn't seem to mind. He was glad to disappear.

*(Joe sits on interior window ledge.
Looks out window)*

There were times I wanted to be dead. There was nothing for me here. It was only when I was nearly dead that I realised I wanted more to be alive.

They used to have dances here... over there.
You can't see it from where you're sitting. Over there.
Wans would come up from the town... I know all about it for I have an interest I ask questions. They like it in here that I ask questions – it shows I'm engaging with the world.

Great dances. Wans come up from the town and everything.
Invite only, tickets were hard to get and everyone wanted a ticket.
The wans in here might have spent all day out in the bog cutting turf.
For the mental had its own bog and its own farm
Wasn't a holiday camp in here ye know, it was not no holiday camp.
All day getting dirty, come back in here to get cleaned up.
Four hundred people getting cleaned up for a dance at the one time
That would be some crack.
The excitement of that, do you not think that would be exciting?
I think that would be exciting...

    (Joe assumes the identity of long dead residents)

HUGH *(rubbing his face)* "James I need a shave, James.
(Listens) Aye I know. You did. Ye shaved me this morning James, but I need to shave again."

PACKIE "James! Paddy's after peeing himself!"

BIG WILLIE *(Speaks slow and low)* "Are you not coming John... never you mind John. I'll come back and tell ye all the crack... Oh there's going to be some crack the night boys!"

PETER *(panicked and distressed)* James, James! Ollie O'Donnell's saying dirty things about weemin. Fuck ye! Hail Mary full of grace the lord is wi me..."

JOE Over on the other side the woman would be combing their hair and putting on lipstick.

God knows between us all we're some assortment. But there was ones in here was handsome too. Plenty in here had no business being here. Boys put in here so their land could be stole off them. Girls put in here because they were pregnant. There were girls in here more beautiful that film stars. Somebody wanted them out of the way.

I'd say they were some ceilidhs.

SMALL CEILIDH BAND MUSIC

> *(Joe in the midst of it all, dancing by himself at the edge of the hall, clapping, watching, responding. He cheers and laughs.)*

Wans were holding hands, swinging round, laughing and shouting.
The floors well sprung, the whole hall bouncing
Plumes of woodbine smoke swirling round...
The smell of sweat and sweet perfume,
Boys o' boys.

> *(Joe slips into the shoes of a gentle dancer, a soft man dancing slowly with his hands by his sides as he gazes lovingly at his partner.)*

DANCER Ye have lovely eyes. Are ye married?
 (Drops to his knees)
 Would you marry me?
 (He is lead away)

> *FADE*

Scene 9

> *(An upstairs window, Joe is following the action below in the car park)*

JOE The sun bouncing off the windscreens
 Irish that for me Seosamh.
 An ghrian ag soilsiú ar an ghloine gaoithe.
 People coming and going, into cars, out of cars, all day long
 Earning the money to make the world go round
 An ghrian ag soilsiú ar an ghloine gaoithe.

 Oh look at her, she's not too happy.
 Nice car and a nice coat but she's not happy.
 Who knows what's going on there?
 For there's nobody diagnosing.
 Nobody assessing them people down there
 To see if they're well or unwell today.
 Look, look, there he goes; into the car, away down town.
 Down round around the roundabout. Traffic and traffic lights.

Back to the auld housing estate, big mortgage, bad auld night,
Dinners not nice, nothing on television, wains won't do what they're told…
He's on a diet, in debt and off the drink. (Chuckles)

I wish everyone in the world was happy. I wish no harm on anyone.
But I'm better off where I am. I can't be getting on with that other stuff.
You wonder then are they happy? It's hard to be happy, hard to be happy.
Irish that for me Seosamh, "hard to be fucking happy".

Cheer up will ye, auld Melancholy Doherty. Tell us all about Melancholy
Doherty, Seosamh. Seosamh wrote a story "Dochartach Dhuibhlionna"
Maybe ye read it. Maybe ye never. Doherty murdered his father – who was
much improved by the murdering process – but it didn't do Doherty no
good. It was a good story.

Ah Jesus Seosamh you should have went to Hollywood instead
of Grangegorman.

Scene 10

JOE   I lived in New York a long time you know.
    You don't believe me, I did.
    Some snow there.
    (Holds hand to describe the depth of snow) Snow up to there.
    Couldn't leave the house.
    Snowbound in the East Village, New York City. Best times of my life.
    Me and Annie looking out the window making up stories
    about the people below… coming and going.

> WE HEAR A RECORDING OF THE VOICES OF JOE AND HIS
> AMERICAN GIRLFRIEND.

ANNIE   "He's just murdered his wife and he's going to the pet store to buy
    piranha fish to get rid of the body".

JOE   "And a king cobra for himself. He'll take it home and stick it in
    the microwave".

ANNIE "He's from a trailer park in Texas can't eat New York food".

JOE "Snake steak and beans".

    (*FADE TO LAUGHTER*)

JOE Snake, steak and beans.

No milk; eating dry sugar puffs, the television dead in the corner. The heating's broken, the plumbing is frozen, shower broke, no money for laundry, we're minging. The smell of your love all over me. Jesus it's freezin'.

Unblock the fireplace and burn a chair. The chimney's blocked, there's smoke everywhere, take an old saucepan nail some holes in the bottom put some coals on the top, fashion a brazier out of that, bake a potato. Open the window let out the smoke, let in the cold.

Dancing to stay warm. New York, New York, doesn't get any better than this.

Christmas dinner, two corn on the cob from a Kentucky Fried Chicken diner.

JOE All I ever wanted to be was free, free to be myself. A fistful of freedom dollars would help. A man has a picture in his head the way he'd like to live his life free from other peoples' shite. I dress as myself so you know it's me.

All I ever wanted to be was free and I was free, I was free, I was free sitting with Annie looking out at the snow.

But you don't know, for you weren't there, you were not. Nobody knows only me and her.

The day after the snow melted I looked out the window;

    (*Looks out window, excited*)

Jesus, Annie, come here – An elephant. Outside the pet store getting its photo took for a publicity stunt; a fucking elephant, in the melting snow, only in New York.

Scene 11

It was a big elephant. Bigger than the ones ye'd see in the circus. They take us out to see the circus whenever it's in town. I'd be a bit embarrassed but I'd still go. You might spot a beautiful woman, but you'd be walking along wi the boys from here; no woman's looking for a man from the mental gang. So I'd pretend to be a nurse, minding them... c'mon boys and hurry up or we'll be late for the circus.

Back in the old days they'd take the whole kit and kaboodle down the town in the one go to see the circus. Everybody that was able. Marching maybe a hundred or more people down the middle of Main Street.

The curtains would be twitching that day.

(Joe mimics a god fearing mother as she pulls her child away from the curtains)

PHILOMENA: "Get you away from thon window or they'll all be looking up"

(The procession begins, marching down Main St. A happy man grows dejected when he is ignored by an old friend.)

MICKY Jimmy, Jimmy, It's me Jimmy...

(Joe mimics the after-mass gossip)

PHILOMENA Oh God aye, I never seen the likes of it in my life. Sure they took up the whole street. If the circus was half as good as that, we'd be at it every night. (Sarcastically) And our friend "You know who", her daughter was there in the middle of them. You told me she was in Strabane. I knew well she wasn't in Strabane, she's been up in the Mental this last three months... if you ask me they have the wrong one from that family up there. The poor wee cretter! I'll say a prayer for her.

(Parade resumes)

And himself from two doors down stop outside his own house and stood looking up at the window. I didn't know where to look, but sure somebody had to keep an eye on him. He went over and started knocking on his own door. They did not open it.

What d'ye mean did the wains see him?

The whole town saw him! How could they not see him! It's a disgrace!

Scene 12

(Joe sits on steps at foot of stairwell)

Billie Holiday. It would be hard to be in the same room as Billie Holliday. I wouldn't be able for it. She's too beautiful. I would be able to look at her or I would be able to listen to her, I wouldn't be able to do the two at the one time. No point pretending I'd be able. Too beautiful. My Annie was like that sometimes... just too beautiful.

> *(Sings)* **Wish I had a queen bee**
> **Buzzing around with me**
> **Wish I had some honey**
> **Life would be sweet**
> **I likes to walk in the garden**
> **And I haven't seen no snakes**
> **Now is the season**
> **When all good heathens need a break**
>
> **All this time I've been wondering**
> **What's been happening with you**
> **All this time I've been wondering**
> **What's been happening with you**
>
> **The storm in my head**
> **The ache in my bone**
> **And all the places in between**
> **All of my day**
> **With no one to hold**
> **Is it so bad for me to dream?**

Scene 13

(Daytime in occupational therapy. Joe is sitting at desk painting.)

JOE I would be influenced by the Tory Island primitive painters.
Only a lot more primitive than that.
Colours is like music. They come right into ye.
(He notices that sensation. Pauses, looks at hands)
They flow right out of ye. *(Stands up watching the colours flowing from his hands)*

It feels good when you let the colour out, like music.
A yellow changing to a green is like an "A7" chord changing to "Em"
Paintings is like windows ye can escape out through them.

(Lights create painting effects)

I can give myself a brand new head
And brand new dancing legs.
I can fill the world with anything I want
I can paint a big green hill... full of daisies

All smiling up at the sun.
I can do another one with the moon
Where all the daisies close their petals except for one
Who's not afraid of the dark... 'cause he has a gun.

Green grass. Mother earth
Look Seosamh, see.
I paint two grass blades
You and me
Standing together, Side by side,
Roots down into the earth. Growing.
The earth is always singing.
Ye have to listen,
Ye have to listen, you can hear the earth singing.
It's scientific
Yeah, yeah
And she loves all her children
Especially the simple ones
And her song can be heard in every living thing
But you have to listen, you have to listen you'll hear her singing

She sings of a time when this place was filled with people from all
over the county, north, south, east and west, our people, and how
they went into the asylum fields to gather potatoes.
Mostly most of them had gathered spuds before,
beyond the walls. For round these parts in them days
As soon as ye walk ye play your part in the purty field.

(Bows moves as if in the potato field)

And bowed before mother earth
The smell of her and the touch of her
Remember then thon place where ye were reared
Remember then your kin.
Stooped here with heads full of memories,
Of potato fields from Ayrshire to Aranmore.
Early mornings and frozen fingers
Tá sé fuar.
Mother earth food on the table...
I'm hungry

Mary, Mary any chance of getting anything to eat?

Scene 14

(Joe moves towards chair)

JOE Ah Seosamh, Do you ever shut up?

Miles Davis, more than jazz (Sits down, plays with his music mantra)
Miles Davis, the birth of cool. John Coltrane, a love supreme.
If it wasn't for music I'd be fucked.
Cab Calloway, Captain Beefheart.
Music is my saviour. Music is my lord.
(Jumps up testifying) Praise the lord!
I'm thinking of starting up a wee band.
I don't know whose going to be in it, but I'll be in it.
I haven't told anyone yet. Ye have to be careful who you tell what you tell.
I have a name for it and everything...
I can't tell ye.

I followed Seosamh till I got to the place where he got stuck. And then I picked him up and I carried him. *(Takes cap from jacket pocket)*

I carry you with me Seosamh. *(Walks to window)*
See the windmills on the hills.
The walls is all gone.
No walls, no chains
No full moon
No wolfmen running around
Only me
Coming to a shopping centre near you soon.
In broad day light. *(Sits at window)*
No shortage of suffering out there Seosamh. They try very hard to hide it.
It takes old warriors like us to grab the nettle by its head.
Seosamh used to have a cap just like this.

(Puts on cap, cheeky big smile, closes eyes, puts finger in his ear, starts to sway and sings)

Is Mise Raifteirí an file,
Lán dúchais is grádh,
Le súile gan solas,
Le ciúnas gan crá.
Ag dul síar ar m'aistear
Le solas mo chroí
Fann agus tuirseach
Go deireadh mo shlí

(After the joviality, he becomes more pensive, takes off the cap and looks at it. Placing the cap on his head and moving slowly towards the chair where Seosamh always sat; he becomes Seosamh, backlit in silhouette with his back to the audience he takes the jacket from the back of chair and puts it on, takes a box of woodbine from one pocket, a box of matches from the other, slowly takes out a woodbine and lights it. Stands proud in the smoke looking stage left, slowly turns to face the audience- all the while in silhouette- puffing away on the woodbine. He leans on chair and grows stooped, slowly sits down stooping towards the floor, stiffly looks behind him stage left, then stage right before sinking down again into stoop)

LIGHTS UP

JOE (*Removes cap and jacket and jumps to feet*) Tell us what you saw Seosamh, what you saw what you never wrote, things there was no words for in any language.

Tell us about the sweet days when ye'd fill your lungs with the sweet air of the world, the sweet air of the sky, and the soft rain softly coming softly down, tell us about Peggy and the puddle, and the water in the puddle, the light of the sky dipping into the puddle, and people you meet and the sky's in their eyes and the sky's in their eyes, and the sky's in their eyes and they're tellin' no lies, they're not trying to hide, and the world in your eyes Seosamh, your eyes, your eyes. I rise. I rise. I rise up some mornings I be so happy I be saying hello to everyone! Hello! Hello! Hello! Hello! How are ye?

Some mornings I be so happy I could skip down town and stop and turn around and say what's the matter wi ye? I'll heal ye wi all the love in my heart. I'll heal the whole world wi the love in my heart.

(*Joe becomes aware of his euphoria and tries to be more controlled*)

Some mornings I feel so happy I'm scared. I'm scared to tell anybody that I feel happy, in case they say there's something the matter with me. "You're very happy today, are you a wee bit unwell? Are you a bit unwell?" No, I'm fucking happy today! You have to be careful who you tell. What you tell.

(*Joe looks at the jacket and cap left untidy on the chair*)

Seosamh look at the state of ye? I can't be telling people I'm looking after you Seosamh. That would be great crack. Somebody would get a bit of overtime figuring that one out Seosamh.

Scene 15

(*Joe lifts his good dogtooth jacket from the foot of the bed and puts it on. Confident and excited in a controlled way, moving a lot, like he was hanging on the corner over twenty years ago.*)

Think I need a wee holiday away from this place
Starts to get to you after a while
Might check myself out.
I can come and go as I please you know.
I might get the 3 o'clock bus to Dublin
Go up to Vicar Street. Some good bands up there, I was never there.
I hear they have good bands.
You lose touch when you are in here a while.
I need to hear some new music.

I played in bands myself you know, I did aye, in New York. Did I tell you
that? I played in lots a bands. The best band I ever played in was the
Mary Duffys.

(Joe walks over to the band and picks up microphone on stand)

1, 2, 3, 4
THE BAND PLAY AT BREAKNECK SPEED
(Sings) **I don't wanna be I don't wanna be crying**
I don't wanna be I don't wanna be dead
I don't wanna be I don't wanna be nylon
I just wanna be I just wanna be thread
And in the night time when you're sleeping
I look at you pretend you're dead
If you O.D there's no point weeping
I'll join the legion and forget
DAMPEN CHORDS

JOE The bass player was Michael O Shaughnesy from Baltimore.
Used to cut himself up. Thought he was fucking Iggy Pop. Half way
through a song he'd stop, drop the bass, pick up a beer bottle, smash
it on the amplifier and drag the broken glass across his chest.
People used to come and see us just for that. Then he'd smile, blood
running off him, he'd pick up the bass and nod.....

1, 2, 3, 4, 1, 2, 3, 4... everybody knows, everybody knows I want you
everybody knows, everybody knows I do
everybody knows, everybody knows I want you
everybody knows, everybody knows I do

My friend Danny Devine owed these boys money. He owed everybody money. They dragged him round the back of a parking lot and shot him in the back of the head.

Scene 16

(Musician sings sean nós while Joe sits on the edge of his bed rocking)

Shantaigh sé lena chuimhne
neamhspléachas an aonaráin
duine nach mbeadh faoi ghéillsine
ag geallúinti an leannáin.

Ach bhí an grá ag síorbhagairt
is thóg sé mar chosaint thart
ar gharbhchríocha an aonarachais
ballai dochta an tsearbhadais.

Is chosain sé go colgach
poblacht an phríobháideachais
is fágadh saor é agus uaibhreach
i stát sceirdiúil an uagnis.

Go dtí gur thimpeallaigh sise é
le diamhrachtaí a scéimhe
is nuair a shéid sí adharca a hacmhainní
bac ar bhac réab ballaí roimpi go réidh.
(*poem by Cathal Ó Searcaigh)

(Rises and walks to window marking out an imaginary room)

Seosamh was in here a good while when he started to get well known for the writing he done before he was here. They gave him a wee room all to himself, put up bookshelves… wi books. A wee writing desk. There you go Joe, go you write a book. But he didn't like it, he only stayed the one night, it was too lonely. He'd rather sit among the hustle and bustle saying nothing to nobody but saying it all by his presence, "I belong among ye. I need to be here with you, I need to be with people".

Go dtí gur thimpeallaigh sise é
le diamhrachtaí a scéimhe
is nuair a shéid sí adharca a hacmhainní
bac ar bhac réab ballaí roimpi go réidh.

(Joe slouches back into the chair, looking at his hands)

The healing is in me now
The music is in me.
Music has the power to heal.

The Temple of Imhotep in Egypt. Memphis Egypt, 5000 years BC they used music to heal people. I saw that on the internet if you don't believe me you can check for yourself.

(Sings) **In the Temple of Imhotep They play some righteous tunes**
In the Temple of Imhotep They play some righteous tunes
In the Temple of Imhotep They play some righteous tunes

Nobody listens to me I'm only an oul' looney.
Fergus used to work in here. He played music.
He's not here no more. Ye'd miss him alright.
I have his number, I might give him a call.

Elgar in the Powick Asylum, the Powick Asylum Band.
I would have liked that, I would have liked that...
That would have suited me.

(Music corresponding to his hand movements in the air)

Putting the notes together. Create language of the soul.
You can hide behind a language or you can allow it be your
truth and let lead you to freedom.
Words to keep our minds busy, so our hearts can be together.

(Self absorbed increasingly intense)

Create harmonic vibrations, invest love into sound waves. Fill all your sound with love. Send it out travelling out beyond. It'll keep going forever and ever. Everything it touches will turn to love. Fill every corner of the room wi the sound of love. And then let the music come into your body and heal ye.

(*Discomfort corresponding to music*) Ye have to be careful. Sound pollution takes up the space where pure sound lives. It poisons the silence. Ye have to fill the space with good sounds so there's no room for bad sounds. Bad sound contaminates the space, destroys pure sound.

Sam Cooke, Mahelia Jackson, Marvin Gaye, Ray Charles, Otis Redding, Jimi Hendrix, Miles Davis, Beethoven, Sibelius, Rachmaninoff, Mozart, Hildegard Von Bingen...

The bad sounds takes up the space where good music should be.

Music can heal ye or music can hurt ye

(Overwhelmed)

You're not allowed to smoke cigarettes when you're standing beside someone in case ye give them cancer.

What about thon fucking radio giving me cancer!

　(*Struggling*)

Evil music noise, music industry, music industry, the industry, world of fear, the power of greed the greed for power, control us all, control the sales, bringing consciousness down, poison music. World of fear, fear of love. No room for love, no room for love... the meek shall inherit the earth... the meek shall inherit the earth, the meek shall inherit the earth... the meek the meek... fucking will not.

Scene 17

JOE Daddy came home drunk
　I woke up
　My mammy was crying
　What's the matter? Didn't I bring you chocolates?
　And he said is my fucking chocolates not fucking good enough for
　ye Mrs High and Fucking Mighty and he flung the chocolates all over
　the floor.

New York is getting too jaggy for me. Bad noises. A lot a bad people in New York. Bad bastards. Danny owed these boys money they came into the bar and dragged him away... I wasn't there... they took him round the back of a parking lot and shot him in the back of the head... left lying dead for three days... Danny, Danny

(Turns to chair)

Seosamh, Look you through my eyes, can ye see?
You know well, look. You know Seosamh.
I was walking up Second Avenue
An old building starts to fall down, they're demolishing it
I want to run and stand under it
To be hit by a falling brick.
To be hit and humbled
Baptised with rubble
And born again
Get compensation. I need money. I need money –
freedom dollars – hot and hungry.
Hauling my stuff from Alphabet city
Up to Hells Kitchen in an old shopping trolley
All my stuff is in there and it looks like I'm a homeless person
But I'm not. I'm not a homeless person, I'm not a homeless person.
I have nowhere to stay just now but I'm not a homeless person
I'm going to stay with friends up in the kitchen
Limping because my left foot is blistered
From wearing a bad auld fucking boot
The wheel buckled – don't worry it's alright, it's alright *(drops to knees)*
These wheels are on fire...

Mammy, mammy

When I woke up in the morning the chocolates were all
over the kitchen floor.

Mammy, mammy

My Mammy was gone. I started to eat the chocolates, I ate them all,
there was more under the armchair, under the cooker, I ate them all
And I puked.

(Standing dusting trousers)

My stepmother Sally wasn't as pretty as my mammy and she wasn't as clever and she listened to stupid shite on the radio all the time.

(Goes right back to the New York trauma)

I was hot and hungry and these boys on the corner started shouting. I can't let them see I'm scared. Don't let them see you scared.

SOUNDS OF THE CITY, SIRENS AND TRAFFIC

And because I'm on adrenaline survival alert I'm super sensitive to sound and I can hear all the bad sounds of the city coming in...I try to keep it out. I know to listen out for the pure sound, fill your head with good sound.

MINK DE VILLE MUSIC BEGINS FAINT AT FIRST BUT BUILDING

I can hear Willy De Ville singing Spanish Stroll on a radio somewhere and I walk fast towards the music. Don't run. I'll be ok if I hear Willy De Ville. The music was coming out of a car pulled up at the sidewalk, but it wasn't loud enough.

So I asked the guy to turn it up, "Excuse me could you turn up the music please" and he did.

(Dances with a joyous abandon and freedom)

Then the music stopped. The bad sounds start flooding in

(Puts hands over ears)

And the cops came. Don't touch me don't fucking touch me

(Lashes out swinging fists and kicking before going foetal under the police assault)

And they bet me and they bet me
(Crouching obviously still traumatised by the beating)
They dragged me to the cells and they drugged me to Bellevue.
I was there for a good while, I think. Maybe I wasn't.
Sally came over from Ireland to bring me home.
(Spent and tearful)
I didn't want to go home. But I wanted to go home. I want to go home

BLACKOUT

Scene 18

→ *(Daytime in the common room, Joe steps centre stage, very sober and tidy)*

JOE I'm alright Mary, aye, I have my coat

I'm going down town today wi Billy. Billy from the occupational therapy.
Going to the guitar shop. Billy said that I need a guitar. *(Fills up with tears)*
Billy and me is going down town to buy a guitar

I'm alright, I'm alright *(Joe pulls himself together)*
I told Billy about my idea for a band he says that sounds like a wile
good idea. He says it might be a bit hard at the start. I'm going to phone
Fergus that used to work here and ask him to help get it going. There might
be a dance up here like they had in the olden days. We'd be playing at it

(Band begins to play softly in the background)

You could come up and dance and I'd be playing
I'd be looking at you and you'd be looking at me and we'd smile at each
other. For I can see you and you can see me
I'm going to call the band "The Chillsville Sanatorium Happy Hour Band"

> *(Sings)* **We're The Chillsville Sanatorium Happy Hour Band**
> **We'd like to invite to come up and dance**
> **The chance of a lifetime**
> **Won't you take a chance?**
> **We're The Chillsville Sanatorium Happy Hour Band**
>
> **We're The Chillsville Sanatorium Happy Hour Band**
> **We'd like to remind to come up and dance**
> **The chance of a lifetime**
> **Won't you take a chance?**
> **We're The Chillsville Sanatorium Happy Hour Band**

THE END